POP-UP
PAPER
ENGINEERING

To my son Ben
with all my love.

POP-UP PAPER ENGINEERING

CROSS-CURRICULAR ACTIVITIES
IN DESIGN TECHNOLOGY, ENGLISH AND ART

PAUL JOHNSON

London and New York

UK   RoutledgeFalmer, 2 Park Square, Milton Park, Abingdon, Oxford, OX14 4RN

USA 270 Maison Avenue, New York, NY 10016

First published 1992
Reprinted 1994, 1995, 1997, 2007

Reprinted 2002, 2005 by RoutledgeFalmer

RoutledgeFalmer is an imprint of the Taylor & Francis Group

British Library Cataloguing in Publication Data
Johnson, Paul
   Pop-up paper engineering : cross-curricular activities in
   design technology, English and art.
   1. Paper. Cutting & folding
   I. Title
   736.98

   ISBN 1-85000-909-0

Designed and illustrated by Benedict Evans
Photography by Bernie Ross and Jez Lugg
Cover design by Caroline Archer
Printed and bound in Cpod, Trowbridge, Wiltshire

CONTENTS

My gratitude to the following schools for allowing me to reproduce their pupils' work:

Beaver Road Primary School, Manchester
Broadheath Primary School, Trafford
Brookburn Primary School, Manchester
Cavendish Road Primary School, Manchester
Reddish Vale Nursery School, Stockport
Richmond Primary School, Oldham

INTRODUCTION

'What I like most about pop-up books is that you know
that all the flat pages will stand up, like real life when you
open them. It's a kind of magic but it's also very clever.'

Mark (aged 10)

Pop-up and movable books hold an instantaneous fascination for children. This book introduces both teacher and child to paper technology in the genre. Traditional and modern techniques of engineering have been adapted so that children at all levels of ability and stages of development can engage in creative paper invention. It is a highly sophisticated language as complex as any domain of science. But basic pop-up concepts are no more difficult to understand than the basics of any other language. Children will discover with the aid of an enthusiastic teacher a whole new dimension of expressing ideas and feelings through paper. The challenge is the often frustrating task of understanding how pop-ups 'pop-up' - for they seem far from logical at times - and the reward, the unparalleled pleasure and sense of achievement experienced when transforming a flat, folded piece of paper into a three-dimensional sculpture. It is in this momentary flowering, from passive horizontality to active verticality, that the desire to learn lies.

At a time when every subject has to justify itself in the curriculum, there can be no other area of technology and design which addresses itself to so many adaptable skills and cross-curricular areas as pop-up work. To start with, paper is just about the most versatile material there is. It can be folded or moulded into almost any shape and is surprisingly strong. A well-worn classroom activity is to make a bridge of paper and to then test it for strength by applying weights. The result can be astounding.

I have seen free-standing paper sculptures over seven metres high which, although weighing no more than a pair of shoes, have the functional strength of more durable materials like wood or metal. At a time of economic expediency, the availability of inexpensive, good quality cartridge paper cannot be overlooked. But there is another kind of economy which is important to schools- that of *space*. As I was once responsible for three-dimensional studies in a school, I am well aware of the nightmare problems in storing sculptural objects. Wherever you put pupils' work, on or under tables, or suspended from the ceiling, it always seems to get damaged. It is here that pop-ups come into their own, for however complex their structure, or large their spatial dimensions, they simply fold down flat like a thin sandwich. This enables pop-ups from a class of thirty-five children to be stored in no more space than that required for the same number of exercise books. The fold-away form also protects art and design work from damage caused by dust, central heating and colour-fading.

It is the Chinese who are credited with the invention of paper, and it is to both them and the Japanese that we are indebted for revealing to us its versatility and mystery. Is it the butterfly-like delicacy of the medium which so reflects the spirit of the Orient? In European pop-up paper engineering we witness the marriage of the two cultures, the holistic unity of the East with the structural invention of the West. But there are two other cultures here, art and science, and in no form do they more harmoniously coalesce than in the three-dimensional book. What is so captivating about published pop-up books is the ingenuity of both story and the realization of the story in paper and artwork forming.

If the language of pop-up engineering is to be internalized, for that is the only way it can have meaning, then one must enter into its mystery. It is a release mechanism for one's innate creativeness for one pop-up revelation inspires another. If it is possible to raise a clown's head into space, then it follows to furnish him with arms, legs and circus environments; and further to apply to those forms hands juggling balls, a bulbus red nose and a wig crowned by a spotted bowler hat. In the foreground could be engineered a seated audience, an icecream seller and the clown's dog. The opportunities for technological inventiveness are endless. Integrated with the visually aesthetic and scientific dimension of pop-up work is the rich kingdom of the literary imagination. Creative writing, the crafted story, is one of the highest orders of linguistic achievement possible. All the children's work described and illustrated here were adventures into storytelling stimulated by paper itself. The more sequential the design of writing, artwork, paper engineering, the greater will be achievements of children, for significant learning is accumulative and developmental. The greatest danger of this book is that the techniques it demonstrates will be 'lifted' out of the context of an interrelated programme of study and given to children as one-off novelties.

What are pop-ups and movable books?

I take a 'pop-up' book to be hinged paper sections attached to book pages in such a way as to lie flat when the book is closed, but which becomes three-dimensional when the book is open. A 'movable' book is one which contains parts which can be moved in some way by using, for example, levers or rotating discs. There are, however, no hard or fast rules about these categories, and some authors use the term 'movable' to include all kinds of engineering including pop-ups. It is not uncommon to find both techniques combined on the same page and for some pop-up sections to have movable parts in them.

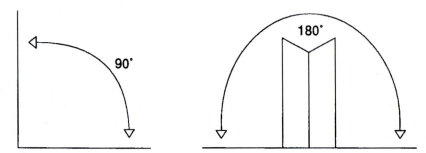

Pop-ups can be divided into two broad categories: those engineered for 90 degree presentation in which pages are raised to the right angle position; and those engineered for 180 degree display in which pages lie flat on the table top.

A pop-up page consists of two parts:

    1) a folded page foundation on which the pop-up parts are attached, and

    2) the pop-up units themselves.

In some types of engineering both parts can derive from the same folded foundation. A sub-division of techniques can be of the paper-cutting and folding methods used. These fall into two kinds:

Single Sheet Engineering: This applies to 90 degree pop-up forms which are cut from the foundation page.

Applied Engineering: Here the pop-ups are made separately and attached to the foundation page.

In some published books the two methods are combined. The basic shapes are cut from the foundation page but additional forms are attached.

Both single sheet and the applied method have their individual characteristics. Single sheet work requires the designer to conceive the whole production before cutting, whereas applied work can, in part, be a trial and error method, as the foundation page remains intact during the designing stages.

Learning about how pop-ups work

Before children can be introduced to pop-up engineering it is essential that teachers are conversant with the language. This is a very practical book designed to help teachers comprehend its grammar. Some children may be well ahead of you in this respect, and then the process is reversed. It is they who will be showing you!

The book has been arranged as a series of workshops, developmental in nature, which are aimed at the classroom teacher. The desire to communicate the art and science of the three-dimensional pop-up to children should arise from a foundation of experience which is both informative and inspirational. The workshops begin with 90 degree engineering forms for no other reason than that it numerically precedes the 180 degree mode of design. There is a 90 degree mentality and a 180 degree mentality, and sometimes both are fused together.

The 180 degree workshop is followed by a brief section on two-dimensional movables. It will be noticed that the forms in the first category out number those of the second. This is because once one passes beyond basic 180 degree forms the methodology becomes increasingly complex. The same could be said for movable book forms but as this is a basic introductory book, more advanced techniques have been omitted. In an attempt to avoid a prescriptive approach, drawing board blueprints are avoided and only occasionally are measurements given. It is understanding the concepts that matter. It makes little difference what dimensions are used as long as the how and why of folding and cutting is assimilated. Only in workshops where the concept is moving towards a higher level of technique is an actual design defined in detail. If something does not work, then ask yourself why. Use the information given in the workshops and your own intuitive inquisitiveness to find the solution.

Curriculum projects - working with children

Following each engineering workshop, suggestions for curriculum activities are given. Like the workshops, these are not prescriptive but aim to stimulate thought about the best way of introducing developmental techniques to children. In many cases the project consists of describing an actual activity experienced by children, and it is for the teacher to adapt this model to his or her situation. There are suggestions for evaluating pupils' achievements and for pupils' own self-appraisals. These are listed under four headings: Conceptualization, Manipulation, Imaging and Visualization.

Conceptualization - here the teacher observes and records the pupils' level of understanding the engineering concepts. This can only evolve from the practical experience of handling and shaping paper, which is conditioned by the ability to control tools. The ability to control tools is the second assessment area - manipulation. In the third area, imaging, evaluation is concerned with children's effectiveness in transforming basic paper shapes into images of meaning, for without form, pop-ups are merely examples of technique. One sees the engineering through the visualised story and the visualized story through the engineering. In this context, language has an implicit role to play, because the way the pupil conceives the image conditions and is conditioned by the accompanying story. Assessment should take into account this related storytelling and writing skill. Finally, visualizing looks objectively at the pupils' skill at enlarging images into art forms. The teacher asks questions about the pupils' developing use of materials, drawing skills, combining colours and textures, and the total design of the pop-up page.

The only meaningful evaluation is one which is intuitive. It is through a growing confidence in one's ability to make and invent pop-ups, an empirical, active knowledge, that curriculum activities are intelligently and sensitively evolved. No set of check lists and testing apparatus can be as effective in assessing what stage children are at, and where they should go next than the intuitively questioning mind of the sensitive teacher.

The curriculum projects must be adjusted to match the conceptual level of pupils. Some will be dexterous with scissors, others will need the cutting done for them. Where cutters are essential, decisions will need to be taken as to who does what. Children do not necessarily have to cut pop-up forms themselves to internalize the concept or procedure of engineering. The projects are structured progressively in cognitive and executive terms. But that does not mean that they must follow one another in sequence. One can move back and forth between 90 °, 180°, and movable techniques because comparable conceptual levels can be found in them. Similarly, selected forms can be engineered at a number of levels of difficulty. The approach to designing projects should be a personal one to suit current classroom themes, projected thematic and topic work, your own predilections or that of pupils' interests and enthusiasms.

The ultimate aim is for children to instigate the pop-up designing, making, evaluating cycle themselves. Some children will be further ahead in some skills than others. Team work, a feature of several projects, brings its own problems and rewards. All in all, I have learnt to be practical and not idealistic in classroom situations like these. One must have the sensibility to recognize when intervention is necessary. The young can have a limited faculty of concentration and immersion in what they are doing. It may be better on occasions to make something for them than to run the risk of losing their enthusiasm because a peculiar technique cannot be grasped.

Cross-Curricular Activities

Most significantly, the projects are cross-curricular in design. There is, to my knowledge, no published pop-up book devoid of text. There is, of course, no reason why pop-up books should be of stories - indeed there are as many of them dedicated to the sciences (pop-up camera, human body, solar system) as storytelling books - it is just that the work of my colleagues and myself with children has fallen into the narrational category. (See recommended reading in the bibliography at the back.)

Visual Arts

I have said little of the role of the visual arts in the movable book genre. Without the dimension of drawing, pop-up books are lifeless shapes. A book could be written showing how children's visual education, critically and expressively, can be developed through pop-up imagery. It requies a very different modus operandi to conventional two-dimensional artwork, for children are required to conceive in both two and three dimensions simultaneously and to package both within a design technology framework. For want of space I have tried to show by example of children's work, rather than by descriptive analysis the inherent stimulus of pop-up work on visual development. 'Dry' colour has been used for artwork (crayon, pencil crayon, pens) as water-saturated materials like paint slow down the assembly process (time to dry) and also crinkles all but heavyweight papers which diminishes the finished appearance of the work. Dry colouring materials have a quality of their own, and it is salutory that international artists like David Hockney, through pencil crayon drawings, have stimulated a revival of these underrated techniques in the last decade or two.

Children have a special relationship with books they have made themselves - particualrly in the case of three-dimensional books where pop-up engineering is interrelated with art and writing in cross-curricular projects. At least, I have always found it so. This area of design education not only motivates those children who by virtue of their intelligence would be expected to respond positively to work of this kind, but also those with learning difficulties. The fact of the matter is that no-one, at any stage of childhood or adulthood, at any level of creative ability, can fail to be moved by the magical stimulus of the three-dimensional book. Children of all ages who discover, empirically, the joy of making their own pop-up books will approach the 'Children's Pop-Up Books' section of a book shop with a maturity and confidence, for they will be able to say 'I know how that pop-up was made because I've invented one like it!'

That is learning of the highest order.

Paul Johnson
Manchester Polytechnic, 1991

Paper Sizes

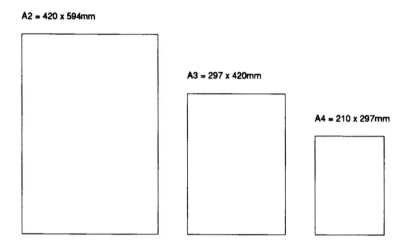

A2 = 420 x 594mm

A3 = 297 x 420mm

A4 = 210 x 297mm

Throughout the book reference is made to three standard sizes of paper: A2, A3 and A4. In the scale above these sizes are given in millimetres for those readers unable to obtain paper in this format.

POP-UP
PAPER
ENGINEERING

What tools do I need?

Before beginning, have ready a pile of (preferably discarded) A4 duplicating paper. As no glue is needed in single sheet engineering, the process of trial and error is simplified. In the early stages of experimentation you will fill the floor with discarded pop-up attempts. Good. This shows that you are really involved in the learning process. Keep sticky paper by you to join mistaken incisions, and, when you feel the time is right, graduate from duplicating to cartridge paper and larger (A3) formats.

The only piece of equipment you need initially is a pair of scissors, but later a cutter will be essential. A cutter is a piece of equipment no design technologist can survive without, for it not only reaches those parts of paper that scissors cannot reach, but also enhances the design process. A cutting mat is also recommended, for it produces a clean, sharp edge to cut paper. Finally, a steel safety ruler will be useful, especially when longer, accurate cutting is required.

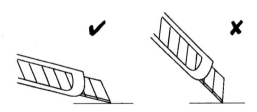

'A cutter reaches those parts of paper that scissors cannot reach...'

1 THE BASIC BOX

'The ability to design is likely to exist already within our pupils, even though it may be largely intuitive and un-organized. They will have ideas for the use of materials and a desire to use them. The vital question is how this can be built upon to bring them to a point where they are able to express their own ides and interests in satisfying creative and competent technical term.'

Schools Council Design and Craft Education Project.

The Basic Box pop-up is one of the simplest forms in the 90 degree paper engineering workshop.

Stage 1: The Basic Box

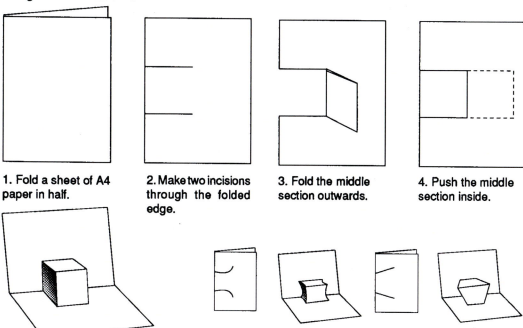

1. Fold a sheet of A4 paper in half.

2. Make two incisions through the folded edge.

3. Fold the middle section outwards.

4. Push the middle section inside.

5. Open the paper to a 90° position.

6. Experiment with the basic form by changing the shape or angle of the cut.

Stage 2: The Four-Fold Base

As experiments develop it will become necessary to adopt a more sophisticated approach to preparing the pop-up page: the four-fold base. The double folded page used in this method is stronger than the single folded page, and therefore more likely to stand up than a single sheet.. It has the added advantage that the blank area behind the negative space of the pop-up can contain artwork. Many people find the final presentation of a four-fold pop-up more aesthetically satisfying because there are no gaping holes.

1.

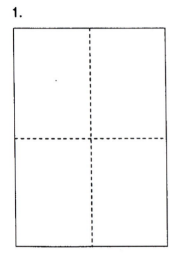

2.

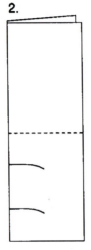

3. **4.**

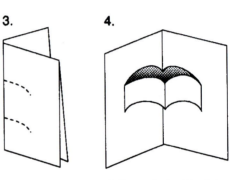

1. First, fold the paper into four equal sections and re-open.

2&3. Fold in half along the vertical. Cut pop-up on the bottom panels. Drop the top panels down behind the bottom panels.

4. Open the inside of the double fold and project the pop-up form.

Dogs
Rose (aged 8)

'Big dogs, small dogs, wide dogs, thin dogs. Dogs that live in the rubbish dump, dogs that live in the street and the nicest place for a dog to live is all snug at home. '

The two orientations of the 90 degree mode.

90 degree forms are capable of being projected in both vertical and horizontal orientations. As you progress you will see that each orientation influences the inherent imagery contained in the form. Thus, a pop-up image conceived in the horizontal will differ from that of the vertical.

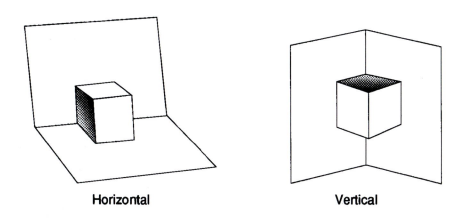

Horizontal   Vertical

'...each orientation influences the inherent imagery contained in the form.'

Points to Remember

Cut lines must always cross the central fold (spine) if designs are to pop up, so the paper must be hinged to the left and right of the fold. If you find yourself cutting a vertical line you are probably making a mistake! Engineering must never be more than halfway across the folded page. If it does, the resulting pop-up will protrude beyond the edge of the page.

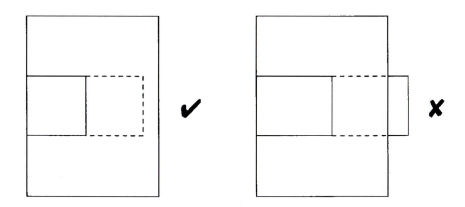

'...the pop-up never protrudes beyond the edge of the closed book.'

1 CURRICULUM PROJECT

Activity 1
|
simulate the Basic Box
|
brainstorm horizontal & vertical themes
|
image and scenario artwork
|
develop storymaking & storywriting

The Box

Experimenting with the basic box technique is a good way for children to begin because a wide spectrum of engineering possibilities are variations of this fundamental form.

Activity 1:

A)   Simply follow stage one described in Chapter 1, developing your measuring and scissor cutting skills. If you have to do the cutting for pupils try to include them in the process. It is important that they watch your demonstration (possibly several times) before embarking on the process themselves.

B)   Brainstorm themes resulting from the box-making activity. 'If this was a shape in a pop-up book what would the story be about?'
One group of eight-year-olds produced the following ideas:

Horizontal Box	*Vertical Box*
Treasure chest	House
Present in a box	Refrigerator
Brick	Tin for holding things
Loaf of bread	Present in a box
House	Garden shed

While most objects relate to only one mode of projection some are conceived in both, for example, the House.

C)   Having determined the image, encourage pupils to pictorialize the form with artwork. Apart from the visual and design skills developed, this task involves children in amplifying the identity of the image. There are two parts to this task: i) artwork appropriate to the image itself; ii) artwork appropriate to the accompanying scenario. This enlarging of the image's concept to include the environment prepares the narrational element of the story-making activity.

D)   Story making. This might come about through discussing the what, where, when of the story structure, programming the object (tree), in relation to the environment (island), at a specified time (one bright sunny day), and an event (whenever anybody wanted to make a wish...). Clearly, Rose's *Wide Dog* illustrated in Chapter 1 will produce a very different story to Beth's *Only Tree* below. What is important is that the simple box form has introduced the class to the mystery of pop-up engineering and the narrational content of story and art which it contains.

The Only Tree
Beth (aged 7)

*'Once there was an island. It had an only tree on it. Whenever anybody
wanted to make a wish they went to the island, climbed the tree & made
their wish. Whatever they wished always came true.'*

Activity 2:

Develop work in activity two by showing pupils how slightly varied cutting patterns can produce very different forms. What images do these forms suggest? What is the story behind them? Pupils can practise scissor-cutting wavy and curved patterns on wastepaper.

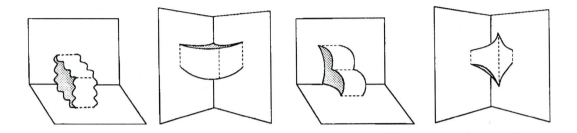

'... practise scissor-cutting wavy and curved patterns on wastepaper.'

'Experimenting with the basic box technique is a good way for children to begin because a wide spectrum of engineering possibilities are variations of this fundamental form.'

Activity 3:

To make the paper form resemble the chosen objects more accurately, experiment by engineering doors and openings. What might be seen through the doors and openings? Ask the pupils for their ideas before drawing an image of what they see on the back panel.

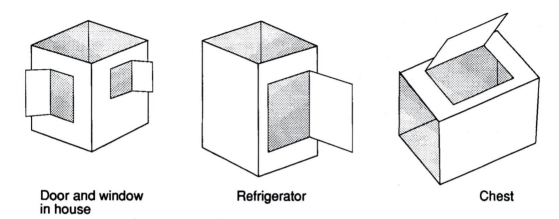

Door and window   Refrigerator   Chest
in house

'What can be seen through the doors and openings?'

Evaluation

Conceptualization: At the end of each engineering activity assess the stage of development of pupils. Progress through the activities only when the basic concepts have been understood through experimentation. Were your demonstrations appropriate to the average ability of the class?

Manipulation: Assess the executive skills of those involved; measuring, cutting (scissor/ cutter work,) folding, projecting. Should more scissor-cutting experiments be made before making the pop-up forms?

Imaging: Assess the image-making and narrational skills of pupils. Did you inject enough imaginative stimulation during the formulating period?

Visualizing: Assess how well pupils related the artwork image of the pop-up to the environmental artwork. Was the range of art materials suitable to the task? How effectively was colour used?

Points to Remember

The curriculum project work so far raises some important questions. For example, does the image grow organically out of the pop-up, or *vice versa*? Although it is legitimate to plan a design in order to produce a predetermined pop-up form, where the beginner is concerned, it is advisable to let the image 'grow' out of the experimental form. It is easier to see an image in a form that has already been made, than to make a form of a chosen image. The simpler the form (the basic box) the more things it can suggest to the child's imagination.

Another issue concerning the teacher is the order that story making/writing/artwork/ design should be introduced. This is a personal affair for both teacher and taught, some teachers operate best when using a systematic model and some children respond best when resolving the arrangements of tasks in their own way. Because pop-ups can never be engineered to the edge of the page (they would protrude if they did) there is always plenty of empty space on which to write and draw. It goes without saying that graphic work should be done on the flat, pushed-down pop-up position. However, a paradox of the genre is that, whilst one designs in the flat, one must conceive in the spatial. The right-angled fold makes all the difference to what is seen. This is an abstract concept which children will become increasingly aware of in their work.

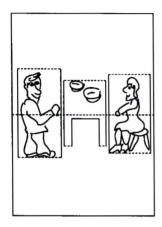

'The transformation from 2D to 3D may distort images.'

'...whilst one designs in the flat, one must conceive in the spatial.'

Encourage pupils to make design drafts in the graphic planning of the pop-up page. Lines of writing are as much part of the design as the artwork.

2 THE BEAK AND HEAD

It is with a degree of caution that the beak form is introduced as it has become a cliché of paper engineering. However, it is logically the same family as the Box and should be included here.

Stage 1: The Beak.

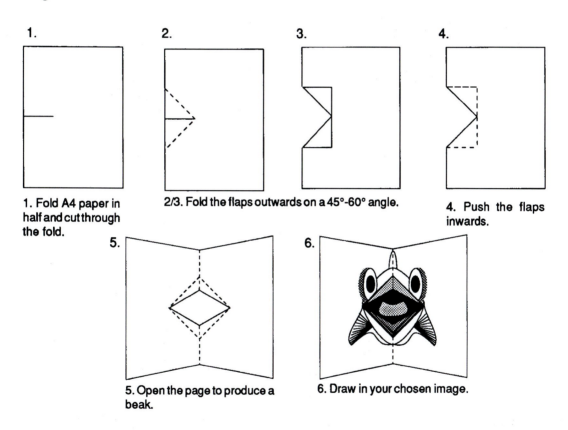

1.

2.

3.

4.

1. Fold A4 paper in half and cut through the fold.

2/3. Fold the flaps outwards on a 45°-60° angle.

4. Push the flaps inwards.

5.

6.

5. Open the page to produce a beak.

6. Draw in your chosen image.

Stage 2: Experiment with the length of the single cut and the angle of folding.

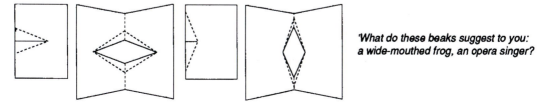

'What do these beaks suggest to you: a wide-mouthed frog, an opera singer?

Stage 3: The Head

A developmental combination of the beak and the box is the Head.

1.

2.

3.

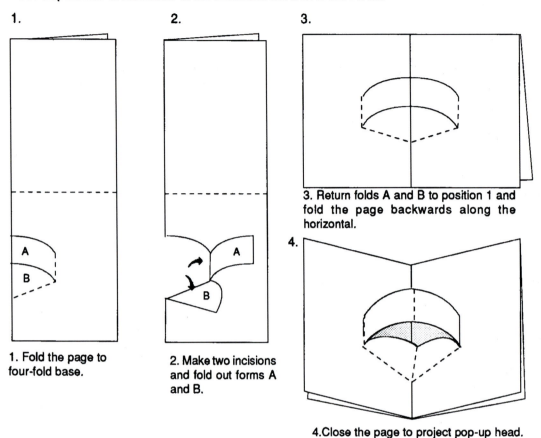

3. Return folds A and B to position 1 and fold the page backwards along the horizontal.

1. Fold the page to four-fold base.

2. Make two incisions and fold out forms A and B.

4.Close the page to project pop-up head.

Stage 4: Eyes

Enrich the basic design by engineering eyes in the main form. As with the Basic Box, and Beak, experiment by changing the contours of the cuts and angles of the folds.

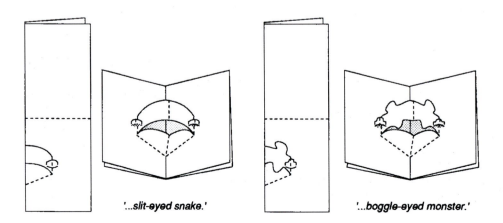

'...slit-eyed snake.'

'...boggle-eyed monster.'

Stage 5: Applied Section

A more sophisticated form of the Head is in both 90 degree and 180 degree modes and requires an applied section.

The Upper Head

The raised head section is engineered on a zig-zag concertina fold (see Chapter 11). This enables the top head section to be raised and lowered on just one horizontal support.

1.

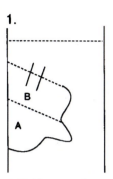

2.

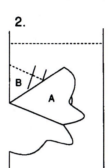

3.

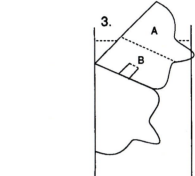

1. Fold page to four-fold base.

2&3.   Cut upper jaw and fold sections A and B upwards.

4. Return folds A and B to position 1. Drop top fold to back. Open page to project head.

Raise eyes

4.

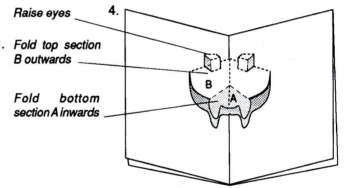

Fold top section B outwards

Fold bottom section A inwards

Lower Head

The only way for the bottom jaw section of the head to be activated is for it to be engineered on a seperate sheet (applied engineering) and glued to the base.

1.

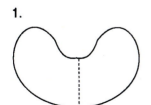

2.

3.

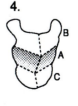

4.

5.

1.   Cut form to correspond to lower jaw.
2.&3. Fold A and B sections as for upper head but project in reverse form.
4.   Fold top section B inwards and bottom section A outwards.
5.   Finally glue panel C in position below upper jaw.

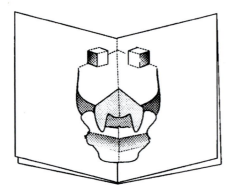

Upper and Lower Head on four-fold base.

'Production of a work is not simply the carrying out of decisions made through definition and analysis. Throughout the actual construction, the designer must remain flexible in order to take advantage of unexpected implications in the material or in the evolving form. It is the degree of imagination with which the necessary choices are made that determines the ultimate character of the work.'

Marjorie Elliott Bevlin *Design Through Discovery* (Holt Rinehart Winston, 1985)

The Gorilla from Jan Piénkowski's *Dinner Time* (Gallery Five, 1981) illustrates the transitional 90 -180 degree opening and closing mouth mechanism characteristic of the upper and lower head method of paper engineering.

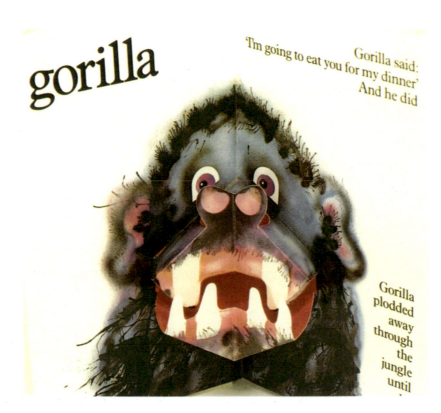

Gorilla
Jan Piénkowski *Dinner Time* (Gallery Five, 1981)

'Gorilla said: "I'm going to eat you for my dinner" And he did.'

2 CURRICULUM PROJECT

Activity 1
|
simulate the Basic Beak
|
discuss emerging imagery
|
cartridge paper realization
|
artwork
|
write in the drafted story

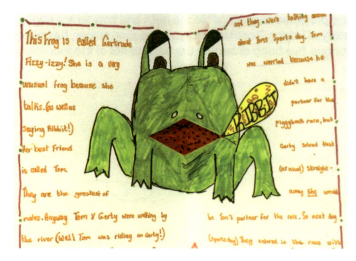

Gertrude Fizzy-Izzy
Jessica (aged 10)

*'This frog is called Gertrude Fizzy-izzy! She is a very
unusual frog becasue she talks (as well as saying Ribbit!)'*

The Beak

The Basic Box project introduces children to the fundamentals of pop-up paper engineering. After experimenting with this form, they will have developed sufficient engineering skills to make the Basic Beak.

Activity 1: The Beak

A)   Engineer the basic beak by following Stage 1 described in Chapter 2. Use your own simulation and blackboard diagrams, and ask the class to experiment with the size and shape of the beak aperture (Stage 2).

B)   As the different beaks emerge, discuss the type of personality that each form suggests. Are some more ferocious than others? Are they real-life or alien creatures?

C)   Progress to cartridge paper and the four-fold base. Pupils can now select one of the experimental beaks for development. After the cutting and folding stages the head/body form can be realized in artwork. But...

D)   remember to allow space for the drafted story/description to be incorporated into the design.

Activity 2: The Head

After communicating the basic cutting and folding techniques of Stage 3 (described in Chapter 2), pursue an experimental period during which children produce several head forms. Once they have grasped this process, progress through the developmental stages of image-making, planning artwork, story-making and drafting, to the final presentation of the design.

The cutting pattern in Laura's pop-up head illustrated below has produced beak-like lips that are projected inwards, while the neck and bow tie are engineered on Basic Box principles. The story of Hoopa Dopolus, the eyeball-eating singer, has been written alongside the artwork. His tongue has been drawn on the back panel of the four-fold base.

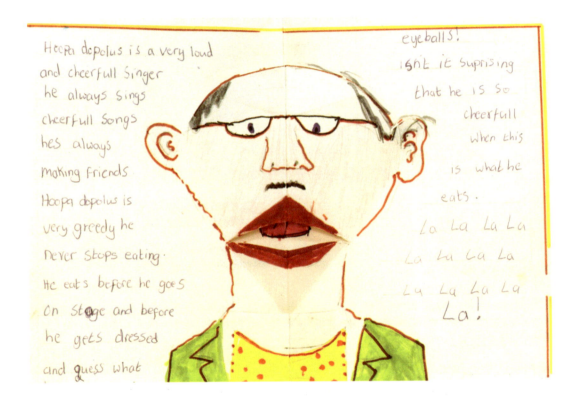

Hoopa Dopolus
Laura (aged 10)

'Hoopa Dopolus is a very loud singer. He always sings cheerful songs. He's always making friends. Hoopa Dopolus is very greedy, he never stops eating. He eats before he goes on stage and before he gets dressed. And guess what - he even eats eyeballs! Isn't it surprising that he is so cheerful when this is what he eats.
La la la la la la la la la la la la la la!'

The Hungry Tiger
Nadia (aged 10)

*'There once lived a hungry tiger who lived in a jungle by a palm tree.
The tiger was hunting for food in the jungle and the tiger saw a
kangaroo. The tiger chased it around. Then suddenly the tiger caught
the kangaroo and ate it up and just left the bones...'*

Activity 3: The Applied Head

The class will need to be guided through the more intricate folding of Stage 5, for the concertina
fold introduces a new way of engineering. When working with children I use an A2 (420 x
394mm) simulation to illustrate this. Working on the large scale, pupils some distance from me
can see the mechanics of the moving parts more easily. Several attempts at making the upper
head form may be necessary and considerable assistance may need to be given to the less
dexterous pupils.

One of the omnipresent dangers of pop-up work - stereotyped forming - is likely here, for
to show children the applied head technique requires from them a certain adherence to your
model. To avoid this, show pupils divergent cutting patterns, for example, different types of jaw,
number and arrangement of teeth, position and design of eyes. Both the image-creating and
artwork stages (B and C) will help to give the evolving head, or creature individuality. The
novelty of the opening and closing mouth is an attractive attribute of the applied head form and
this should be used to stimulate the emerging story (D). Is the creature yawning? If so, why?
Has he just eaten something he shouldn't have? Nadia's Hungry Tiger illustrated above is one
example of the applied head form.

Evaluation

Conceptualization: The task here is to assess whether or not pupils have grasped the transforming 2D/3D principles. If the box technique of Curriculum Project 1 has been understood, then the head engineering of Activity 2 should lead logically into applied head engineering. Did you adequately sequence the cutting and folding stages? Did you ask questions like, 'What do we do next?' Could a successful engineer have been engaged in helping others? Who were struggling?

Manipulation: Assess the developing ability to cut and fold accurately. Did pupils grasp the concertina fold of the applied technique?

Imaging and Visualizing: This project demands richer and fuller images in the context of artwork and story-making. Are pupils fully exploring the visual potential of their pop-up characters?

Pupil Evaluation: Invite individuals to state what they found most difficult in the project. Could some tasks have been made easier? If they made another one, how might it be different? This analysis can then be written up in the form of a design-brief notebook, in which pupils record their work critically and make suggestions to support engineering work in the future.

3 THE RISING ARMS

The Rising Arms form is really a post script to the first two chapters. It is a very basic structure and could be integrated almost anywhere in the developmental designs of the last few pages. Although both the examples given here are of rising arms, this pop-up form could equally easily suggest other images: for example, the fins of a fish, the wings of a bird, or even the legs of a dancer.

1.

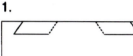

1. Cut wedge-shapes on the fold to form arms.

2.

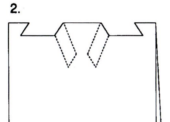

2. Fold the wedges to the inside.

3.

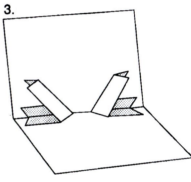

3. Open the page to raise the arms.

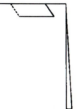

Amaryllis Astonbury is always on a diet. She is really into keeping fit and runs twenty miles per day. Last year she was nominated for the Exercit of the Year Award.
She is an Australian lady who lives on Mt. Everest, supposedly for her health, but she is forever having colds. In spite of this, she continues training.
She is a vegetarian and she does not drink alcohol.
She has two meals a day which consist of half a lettuce leaf and some soya beans But she is still quite chubby. She is quite cheerful too

By D. Cammack (10)

Amaryllis Astonbury
Daniela (aged 10)

'Amaryllis Astonbury is always on a diet. She is really into keeping fit and runs twenty miles per day. Last year she was nominated for the Exercise of the Year Award. She is an Australian lady who lives on Mt. Everest, supposedly for her health, but she is forever having colds. In spite of this, she continues training.
She is a vegetarian and she does not drink alcohol. She has two meals a day which consist of half a lettuce leaf and some soya beans. But she is still quite chubby. She is quite cheerful too.'

3 CURRICULUM PROJECT

simulate the Rising Arms
|
discuss narrative imagery
|
artwork
|
write in drafted story

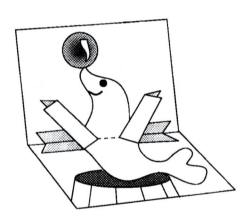

The trip out

...eday a man who was called Mr Brown said to his ...ild who was called Polly. "It's time you learnt to ...wim." He took Polly to the swimming baths. Polly put on ...er swimming suit and her swimming cap and went into

...the pool. Her dad followed. Her dad showed her ...ow to do the breast stroke. Polly found the arm ...ere very difficult but she found the legs very ...asy. But soon she had got the hang of it ...cept on going. Polly did a whole width.

Jennifer 1

The Trip Out
Jennifer (aged 8)

'..although the engineering skills are minimal, the resulting language and visual results may compensate for it.'

'Polly put on her swimming suit and her swimming cap and went into the pool...Her dad showed her how to do the breast stroke...Polly did a whole width.'

This technique can be used as an interlude between more demanding forms of 90 degree engineering. Whilst it is a very basic form suggesting raised arms, I have known it to generate a wide range of figurative images from children of all ages. It is therefore very suitable for capturing the imaginations of younger children just entering the pop-up domain. It stimulates ideas suggesting people clapping or waving their arms, and this in turn results in narrational development. Something as simple as this may inspire children to write something in a way that more orthodox starting points would fail to do. So, although the engineering skills are minimal, the resulting language and visual results may well compensate for it.

4 TOY THEATRE I

'There is a strange preconception in many branches of education that two-dimensional work is a necessary precursor to modelling, building and working; on consideration, the opposite is more logical for many children and adults. The foundation for knowledge and learning is laid on direct experience of our very three-dimensional world. Buildings, furniture, household effects, vehicles, toys, machines - are all three-dimensional phenomena.'

Margaret Morgan *Art 4-11* (Basil Blackwell, 1988)

The Toy Theatre is the classic horizontal 90 degree pop-up book. Its popularity in the three-dimensional book genre is reflected by the many variations of the Toy Theatre discussed here. First, I shall describe it in its simplest form. From here onwards, a cutter is essential because incisions will be made in the flat opened page and not across the folded spine.

The Swan illustrated below combines pop-up paper engineering, artwork and poem by ten-year-old Joanne. A beautiful example of interrelated skills.

The Swan
Joanne (aged 10)

'Swan gliding down the stream,
How gracefully you move.
Your two black eyes like diamonds
gleam,
The water makes no groove.

The water is clear,
The water is cool.
Swan you come very near
In your very own pool.'

Stage 1:

1.

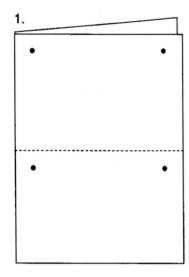

2.

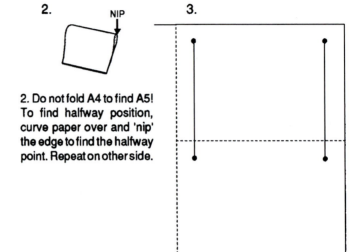

NIP

2. Do not fold A4 to find A5! To find halfway position, curve paper over and 'nip' the edge to find the halfway point. Repeat on other side.

3.

1. Fold A3 to A4. On right panel mark 2cm down from top and in from the left and right sides. Repeat from halfway posistion.

3. Open A4 to A3 and cut vertically between the two points on the left and right sides.

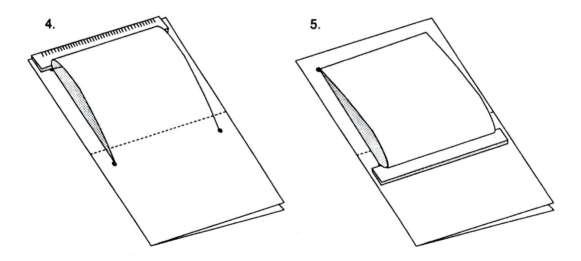

4.

5.

4. Refold A3 to A4. Raise central panel and crease along top edge. Lay ruler above fold to avoid tearing.

5. Repeat creasing along bottom edge of panel.

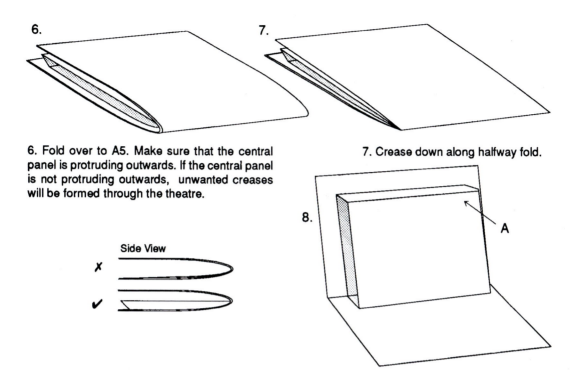

6.

7.

6. Fold over to A5. Make sure that the central panel is protruding outwards. If the central panel is not protruding outwards, unwanted creases will be formed through the theatre.

7. Crease down along halfway fold.

8.

A

Side View

✗

✔

Points to Remember

8. Open to project the theatre.

Pop-up fold 'A' has been creased automatically by the folding down process. It does not protrude beyond the top of the page when closed because its 2cm depth parallels the same measurement below the half-way point. It is essential to understand this principle if developmental complexities of the theatre style of projection are to be successful.

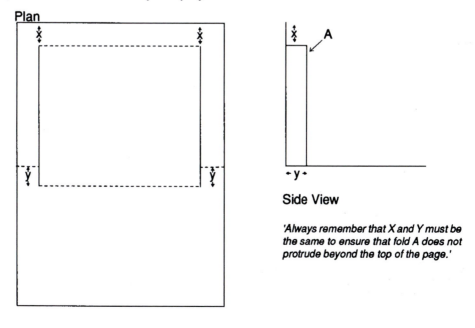

Plan

A

x

x

y

y

Side View

x

y

'Always remember that X and Y must be the same to ensure that fold A does not protrude beyond the top of the page.'

Stage 2:

This involves cutting out the archway opening of the theatre.

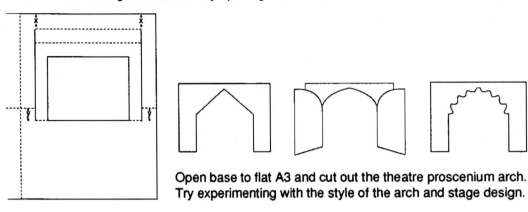

Open base to flat A3 and cut out the theatre proscenium arch.
Try experimenting with the style of the arch and stage design.

Stage 3:

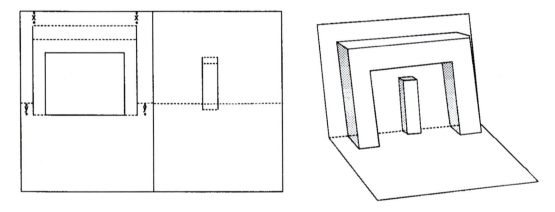

Open the page out flat and reverse. On the centre of the right panel draw two parrallel lines 1cm below the halfway point and rising to just below the proscenium arch. Add 1cm to top of form and engineer towards you, as described in Stage 1 overleaf, steps 4-6. Fold back into the theatre again. The pop-up form represents a figure on centre stage.

Drawbacks

• The negative space created by the figure is visible on the outside of the base. (This can be hidden if the theatre is bound, a process described in Chapter 10.)
• There is an unwanted fold 1cm up from the figure's base. (Later it will be shown how this can be avoided.)

Stage 4:

Experiment with the forms of engineered figures, objects and interiors. Even the smallest alteration can be dramatic. A simple square can suggest anything from a table to a treasure chest, while the addition of a curve or the change of an angle introduces a whole host of possibilities: a tree, a balloon, or a magic toadstool...

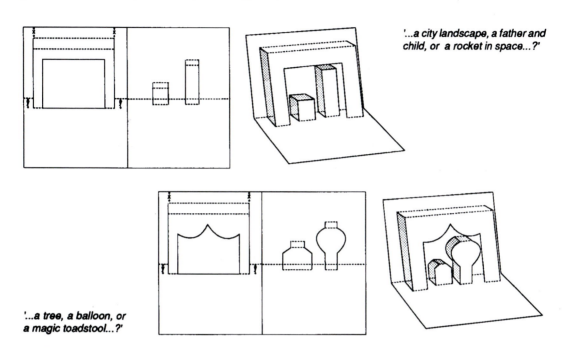

'...a city landscape, a father and child, or a rocket in space...?'

'...a tree, a balloon, or a magic toadstool...?'

Two variations on the 'Snow White' theme
Lisa and Rachel (aged 6)

'Both theatres illustrate the intuitive way in which young children use colour and coordinate verbal and visual images. Lisa has presented her story in book form attached to the theatre's foreground. Rachel engineered her prince on the outside of her theatre.'

4 CURRICULUM PROJECT

'...design is unique: no other subject can so successfully bring together the separate strands of science, arts and social studies in a way that is relevant and appropriate today. Design, in the sense of the process by which we adapt our environment creatively to meet our needs, is the key to understanding many of the problems and opportunities facing our society.'

Ken Baynes *About Design* (Design Council Publications, 1976)

Toy Theatre
Debbie (aged 8)

'Debbie performs her toy theatre production "Chang Wong" to a captivated audience.'

The Toy Theatre I offers a model of cross-curricular activity embracing paper technology, visual design, story-play making and performance. In the following pages I describe a curriculum project carried out with a class of 8-year-olds.

Toy Theatre

A)   Making the theatres

The toy theatres were made prior to the first activity period. The skills required in making them were beyond the average ability of the children and I justified this *fait accompli* approach because I knew that the stimulus of the theatre would generate enormous commitment and learning in other ways. I used the 'Multiple Making' technique, as I call it, to make the thirty odd theatres as quickly as I could. This method comprises holding four (or more) base sheets together using bulldog clips, laying a card master on top (the same cutting pattern as in Stage 1 (3)) and cutting through all sheets simultaneously. The theatres have to be assembled individually but it is astonishing how quickly one can do this after about the fifth theatre. With older pupils I would have cut the two parallel lines myself, but the folding out stages would have been done by them. Progressively, one would expect the whole process, including the initial measuring and cutting, to be done by pupils.

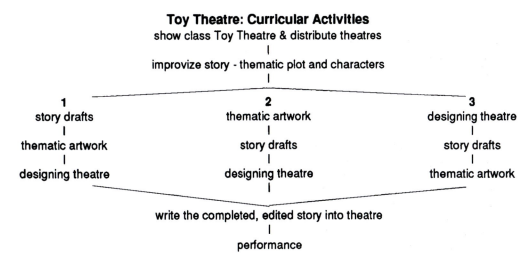

Toy Theatre: Curricular Activities
show class Toy Theatre & distribute theatres

improvize story - thematic plot and characters

1	**2**	**3**
story drafts	thematic artwork	designing theatre
thematic artwork	story drafts	story drafts
designing theatre	designing theatre	thematic artwork

write the completed, edited story into theatre

performance

B)   Stimulating the class

I sprung a nineteenth-century toy theatre on the class and the magic of the 2D-3D transformation took their breath away. There was a momentary silence before a torrent of questions about how it was made was aimed at me. The ready-made toy theatres were distributed so that each child could see them at close quarters, but, more especially, identify with them, for these theatres were now *theirs*.

C)   Thematic exploration

Brainstorming themes, characters, plots and events now took place. The Chinese New Year was upon us, so this was taken as our general starting point. Reflecting on landscapes - rivers, mountains, palaces, forests and waterfalls - I improvized a story with them about an imaginary boy called Chan Wong who 'had all kinds of wonderful, strange and magical experiences'.

D)   Developmental Strategy

The class was now given three choices of procedure.
1.   To write their story in drafted form. This was for those children who had formulated a story and wanted to write it down.
2.   To draw the background scenario and pop-up character. Some children preferred to do the artwork first and let this process of visualization feed the imagination with ideas. (This project used the applied technique of engineered figures described in Chapter 6.)
3.   To design the theatre décor. For those children who had not formulated any kind of imagery, the proscenium arch provided a positive starting point. Whilst those in the other two categories were developing their stories in writing or artwork, I could concentrate on those in this third category, and elicit stories individually.

E)   Completion

The writing of the final draft into the theatre foreground followed, and in some cases this extended to the back page. The final task was the cover design including title and author/ designer.

F)   Performance

This was developed in four stages.

1.   Rehearsing the story only. This was best memorized because in performance the writing is projected away from the performer and thus is upside down.
2.   Performing story to partner.
3.   Performance to class.
4.   Performances taken 'on tour' to neighbouring classrooms of younger children.

General Hints on Designing the Theatre

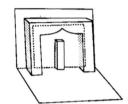
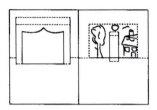

1. Cutting too near the edge of the theatre arch will weaken it and cause it to collapse.

2. Draw outline of theatre space through to backdrop. It is pointless to fill rear panel with scenario artwork when only half of it will be seen.

3. Draw scenario on inside page and not through proscenium arch. Check scenario through arch regularly to review balance of design. The main character should stand out well and be complemented by the background. Draw in stage floor if wished.

Explore ways of arranging design and writing:

1. Writing on front panel.
2. Foreground audience, story on the cover.
3. Story presented in book form.

1.   2.   3.

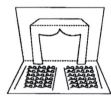

Evaluation

Conceptualizing and Manipulating:	As pupils were given the theatres ready-made, the conceptualizing process was one of inspiring them to want to make their own examples. At the end of the project they actually did this, and this led to developmental work. My evaluation consisted of assessing the level of enthusiasm for making the engineered parts themselves.
Imaging and Visualizing:	This consisted of comparing the written stories with their pictorialization in the theatre. I wanted to assess how the two had been coordinated. This was done through a discussion period. Most pupils said that they worked out the story first in their heads and then 'drew it in', as one child put it. We looked at the theatres. I asked 'How could we have made the backgrounds more interesting without interfering with the pop-up figure? What colours could we use to make important objects stand out and less important objects look less important?'
Performance:	One of the most significant parts of the project was the critical attitudes of pupils when listening to each other perform. Comments ranged from 'It's too long,' to 'You're not holding the theatre still when you talk'.

5 HORIZONTAL FORMS

'The special value of design thinking as a learning tool is that the child is obliged to use intellectual powers on concrete matters and the implications of his thinking and decision making cannot be lost in the recesses of his mind. Design decisions (the consequences of design thinking) will exist in material form in front of the child and his teacher and it is this concreteness which gives design thinking its particular value.'

Richard Kimbell *Design Education* (Routledge & Kegan Paul, 1982)

'The secondary pop-up form leads on quickly to the tertiary form...'

The pop-up structures described in this chapter are all developments of the Toy Theatre. The Shopfront, Piano and Fireplace (picutred overleaf) illustrate the different ways in which the basic theatre shape can be enhanced, and show how secondary pop-ups can be engineered out of main (primary) forms. The techniques used are a simple step from those described in Curriculum Project 4. The secondary pop-up form leads on quickly and easily to the tertiary pop-up form as more and more possibilities unfold. From the basic three-tier structure a class can make anything from a doorstep to a wedding cake - or, in the case illustrated in the following pages: a piano, its keyboard and a stool.

Example 1: **Shopfront**

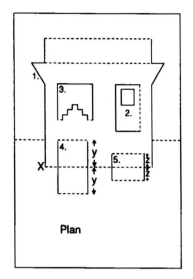

Plan

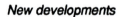

Side View

Shop Counter
Box
Doorstep

Detail: Rear view of shop counter 3. Drops down to form the counter and is glued to the back of the shop.

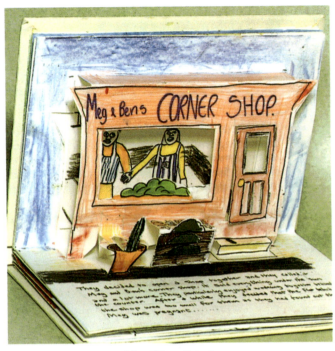

The Shopfront

New developments

1. Rather than a straight vertical line defining the shopfront, an ornamental architrave has produced a more interesting design.
2. A hinged door with cut-out window adds the dimension of a movable part to the facade.
3. The window pane has been engineered back into the shop interior producing a window display and a horizontal shop counter.
4,5. Both the box and doorstep are secondary pop-ups engineered out of the primary (shop front) pop-up.

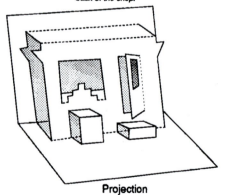

Projection

Secondary pop-ups

In this first example of secondary forms the existing bottom fold of the primary form 'X' is used as the outer fold of the box and doorstep. This necessitates both measurements 'Y' to be the same, and both measurements 'Z' to be the same so that a squared form is created. It is not possible to raise the two forms using the standard technique, so new, dexterous techniques are demanded. If one's little finger is too large to raise items like the doorstep, a pencil or nail might be useful here.

Example 2: **Piano**

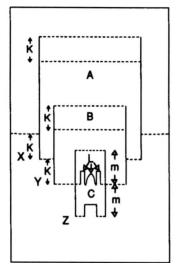

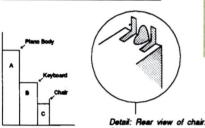

Detail: Rear view of chair. Showing positive vertical forms and resulting negative spaces on horizontal chair seat.

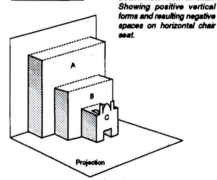

Projection

Engineering Strategy

The Piano

New developments

1. Tertiary pop-ups engineered out of secondary pop-ups.
2. Vertical extensions engineered out of horizontal areas.
3. Separate folding of primary, secondary and tertiary forms.
4. Chair mouldings L rise above seat C, but do not protrude beyond edge of page when folded flat.

The tertiary pop-up C (piano chair) is engineered out of B (keyboard) which in turn is engineered out of the primary form A (piano body). An important new development is that the base of the primary form X does not cross the whole area but left and right sides of the piano body only. Parts B and C subsequently continue the bottom horizontal fold but on their own levels - Y, Z. The implication here is that it is impossible to engineer the primary form A without simultaneously raising forms B and C. The top fold of the primary fold K is unaltered. Therefore, fold K as Toy Theatre I, but fold XYZ separately. Before lowering down to closed position, ensure that 'L' (chair back mouldings) are in the raised position. This is to avoid creasing them. Crease the top flaps of the keyboard and chair to help the folding into position process.

Example 3: **Fireplace**

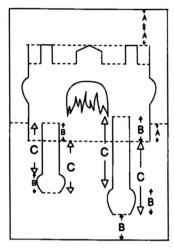

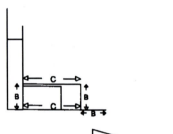

The Fireplace

New developments

1.   Ascending extensions on primary forms
2.   Elongated secondary forms.

This example also shows how secondary (and indeed tertiary) forms can project some distance from their primary source, providing that the height of that form is no greater than the remaining space of the page base in front of it. To reiterate, distances B must equate each other on the forms and distances C likewise.

Engineering strategy

The candlesticks and clock on the mantlepiece are engineered as extensions in the same manner as the chair mouldings in Example 2. But as they rise upwards out of the top of the primary form an extra depth must be provided to prevent them sticking out of the closed page. Therefore two equal distances 'A' must be left uncut above these ornaments. The price to pay for this decorative contour is that the primary form has to be shorter to compensate for it.

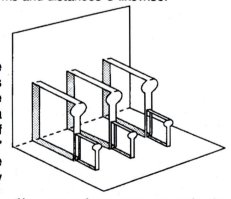

'Now start to invent your own explorative form...skittles, a pier, or a troop of dancers?'

5 CURRICULUM PROJECT

Meg and Ben

Meg and Ben were in love. They got married and there was an enormous wedding cake...

This is the church they were married in. It had stained glass windows and two tall steeples...

They decided to open a shop together. It was called Meg and Ben's Corner Shop.

They bought a house. It wasn't far away from the shop. It had a big stone fireplace in the lounge.

A baby was born a few months later. It was a girl. When she grew older Meg and Ben bought her a piano.

Ben made her a treehouse because she loved climbing...They would all go up the tree and talk. The End.

The illustrations above show a group pop-up book produced by five 10-year-old children. Some of these forms have been analysed in the previous workshop. Instructional plans were used to communicate the more complex operations and the teacher was closely involved at all stages. Curriculum Project 5 is a simplified version of the one above, but still involves children working from drawing plans. Ideally, children should make their *own* design plans, but the necessity of comprehending the abstractions of engineering sometimes demands a prescriptive approach. In developmental projects the creative instinct and inventive desire should produce designs which are wholly personal in character.

Preliminary Stage

make line plans
|
duplicate
|
prepare toy theatres

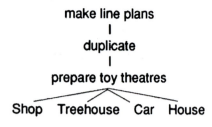

Shop   Treehouse   Car   House

Pre-activity:

A)   Make plans of four explorative horizontal forms. Base your ideas on those already explored in the previous workshop, but adjust them to the ability level of the pupils. Some suggestions for plans are given below. Make them more simple or more complicated according to the pupils' conceptual level. Draw boldly in black pen on A4 paper and duplicate copies as necessary. Then make models of the four forms you have chosen to use as examples.

B)   Prepare A4 Toy Theatres for the whole class simply by cutting the parallel lines. Always make more than are needed.

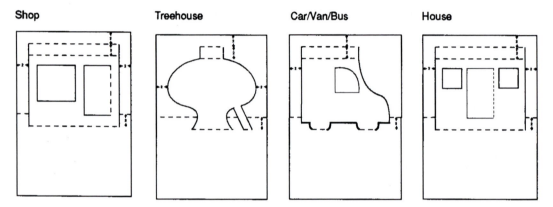

Shop   Treehouse   Car/Van/Bus   House

'Make the plans more simple or more complicated according to the pupils' conceptual level.'

Activity 1
|
demonstrate initial folding
|
process second assembly
|
distribute plans
|
engineer pop-up
|
transfer plan to cartridge paper
|
develop group story plot
|
artwork design
|
written presentation
|
assemble book

Activity 1: Basic Engineering

A)   If possible, stagger the introductory period so that two groups of four pupils can be grouped together. Demonstrate the Toy Theatre I cutting and folding techniques.

B)   Distribute uncut A4 paper and initiate the measuring and cutting procedure followed by the folding technique once more.

C)   Distribute your ready-made plans to the class. Show your own pop-up models pressed down flat *and* in a three-dimensional position. Refer to the comparable parts of the children's plans as you do so. Describe and demonstrate the various aspects of engineering appropriate to their brief, but omit a deeper analysis at this point. The aim here is to get them started on the making process.

D)   The group now cut the vertically orientated lines on their plans (using steel safety rulers where possible) and engineer the primary form building on the experience they gained in stages B and C above.

E)   Distribute A3 cartridge paper. Pupils fold in half to A4, carefully aligning corners before creasing down the centre. They now transcribe the flattened-out plan to folded cartridge using a pencil. Discuss measuring and layout.

F)   Now cut and fold the design and move to a three-dimensional position.

Activity 2: Story Making

Brainstorm the characters and the plot of the story, linking the four objects together. As a preparation for this, write the four objects on cards, jumble them up and improvize a story with the pupils which logically (albeit surrealistically) interrelates them into a whole. Re-mix the cards and improvize a new story.

shop/car/house/treehouse

will produce a very different plot to:

car/treehouse/shop/house

At this stage only a story outline is necessary. The detailed development can be done later. The aim is to establish a plot sufficient to start the visual identification process. (The group story book, 'Meg and Ben', illustrated overleaf shows how six randomly-selected forms were made into a linked plot.)

Activity 3: Artwork

The artwork should follow a similar process to the one described in Curriculum Project 4 (Toy Theatre I). The artwork is of two kinds: i) exterior (primary pop-up) forms, ii) interior, background design on the back page. As before, it is necessary constantly to open the pop-up and visualize the inside as it is seen in a three-dimensional position.

Activity 4: Story writing

As artwork is completed, it is time to return to the story and to develop it in written form. The content of all, or some, of the four episodes may well have changed through the influence of the transformative process of artwork realization. Drawing in a landscape or filling out an interior can introduce new ideas to the sub-plot and thus modify the corporate story. In order for the sequences to correlate smoothly it is necessary for each individual to be familiar with the connecting story plots. In the drafting and editing process, parts may occasionally need to be rewritten so that one continuous piece and not four fragments emerge. Another important consideration is the story length. The page space available for this varies according to the area covered by the pop-up on the bottom panel. In some cases this is three-quarters of the page - in others less than half. Some episodes may need contracting to fit the space.

Activity 5: Final assembly

When all book pages are complete, the final task is to bind them together by glueing the pages in sequence. The card cover should be 0.5cm larger than the book pages on left side, top and bottom, but flush to the spine. Score approximately 2cm spine on outside of cover. (For a description of more professional binding methods, see the list of books in the bibliography at the back.)

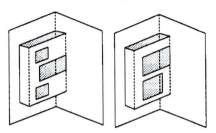 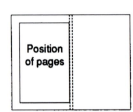 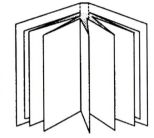

Glue pages back to back.

Position of pages

The diagram above shows the book in its vertical position: when it is 'read' it is, of course, in the horizontal position.

Evaluation

Conceptualization: In this project pupils are introduced to the basic language of 90 degree engineering in a series of graduated stages. Some processes are repeated, but each time a new element is incorporated into it. Children working from a plan and then drawing the plan themselves before engineering it is an important new step in the acquisition of paper technology skills. Assessment - keep a record of pupils' skills in the developmental cutting, folding, engineering, technical drawing exercises. How accurate was the measuring? Did pupils grasp the essential concepts of folding? What did they find hardest and how might this part of the project be reconsidered in future?

Manipulation: The executive dexterity required by this project is demanding on patience. Could the folding process be simplified? Were there too many cutting and folding sequences resulting in a loss of enthusiasm?

Imaging: The group technique of providing a story involves interpersonal skills of communication. Some children may respond to it better than others, and some may dominate the improvisory exchanges. Assessment - were the four participants all actively engaged in making the story? Did they help one another ? Was as much interest shown in the writing activity as the other parts of the project?

Visualizing: How might you assess whether or not the pop-up forms stimulated enthusiasm for the artwork? Are all parts of the design equally arresting? If not, how might pupils be stimulated to see the whole of it as a total design?

There is ample opportunity in this project for periods of self-assessment, for each episode is a complete unit as well as a link in a chain of events. A description of encountered problems can be recorded in a pop-up design journal, together with suggestions for developmental progressions, engineering and thematic ideas. Pupils can make a list of 'what I liked' and 'what I didn't like' about the project - useful in planning projects in the future. Above all, the intention of the project is to lead pupils towards the skill and confidence they need to design their own explorative pop-up structures.

6 APPLIED FORMS

Rocky v Darago
Ian (aged 10)

'In this picture Rocky and Ivan Darago are fighting for the World Championship in USSR.In this picture Rocky has hit Ivan Darago against the ropes and he has fallen flat on his back. The referee has counted up to ten and in the end Rocky has won by a knockout.'

Most of the engineering examples so far have been of the single sheet kind - nothing structural added or taken away from the engineered page. By *applying* forms, a pop-up design can be made more interesting without the gaping holes left by the single sheet method. Rocky and Darago (pictured above) are both examples of applied forms. This left the back panel free for a drawing of the boxing ring. Ian's reportage of a real-life boxing match also shows how the toy theatre model can accommodate thematic material from any subject.

Applied figure for Toy Theatre I

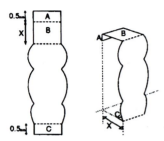

Turn back folds 'A' and 'B' over figure and glue fold 'A'.

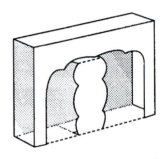

1/2. Design figure to be no taller than the height of the proscenium arch. Add to figure height extensions to folding 'B' and attaching 'A/C'.

Flap 'B' must be the same width as the distance between the figure and the back of the theatre 'X'.

3. Lay figure face downwards and glue base 'C' to position in the theatre.

5. Project theatre and figure.

4. Drop theatre down, 'A' will find its own position on the theatre's rear wall.

Experimenting with applied forms

Applied forms can be built on to pop-up structures whenever they are felt necessary and can effectively co-exist with single sheet forms. Here, two applied forms are constructed over a single engineered 'box'. The figure has been made in two sections (body and supporting strip). The supporting strip has been glued to the middle of the applied figure, thereby making it less obtrusive.

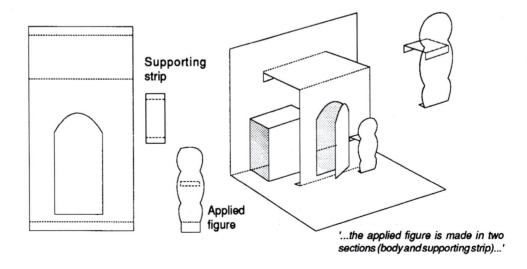

Supporting strip

Applied figure

'...the applied figure is made in two sections (body and supporting strip)...'

7 VERTICAL FORMS

The main difference between the logistics of vertical and horizontal engineering lies in the design of the subject-matter. This is a distinction that affects the engineering concept substantially, for structures conceived in the vertical need to be redesigned if they are to exist in the horizontal.

Example 1: **Automobile**

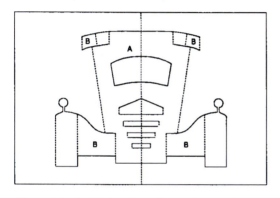 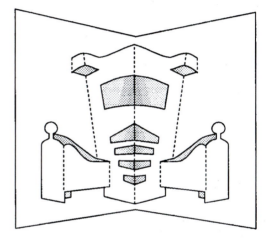

'The car's body 'A' is the primary form and the mudguards, wheels and roof 'B', secondary forms.'

There is a technical advantage to the vertical mode. As the design tends to lie centrally both sides of the central fold can be cut simultaneously as in the basic 'beak' forms. This simplifies the technique, particularly for the beginner. Of course there is no reason why both sides should be symmetrical and indeed to make the design more interesting this should be avoided in developmental work.

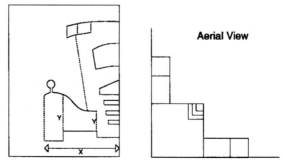

'The rule that engineering must not protrude beyond the half-way point of the page is no longer relevant. The secondary folds 'Y' enable 'X' to extend significantly beyond that point.'

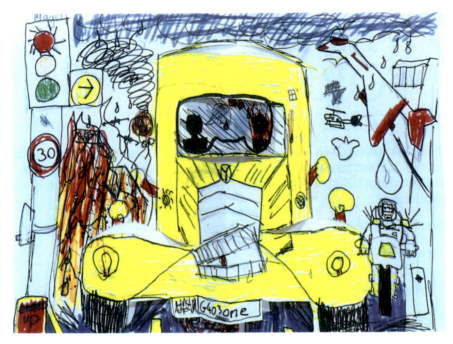

The Run-away Car
Buda (aged 11)

The Run-away Car is a simplified version of the Automobile described in Example 1 overleaf. The whole windscreen section is a pop-up inversion. The story of the run-away car is written on the back of the page.

Example 2: **Mystical Mountain**

This is a more complex design than the Automobile described in Example 1. The conical primary form 'X' has secondary forms 'A' engineered as swivels. 'Y' is a pop-*in*, the angles of which enable the 'A' forms to protrude outwards. Forms 'Z' perform a similar function, enabling the front portions of the 'A' forms to project outwards and the inside portions to recede into the conical primary form, thus creating a swivel action.

Plan

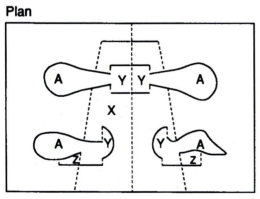

'The conical primary form 'X' has secondary forms 'A' engineered as swivels.'

Projection

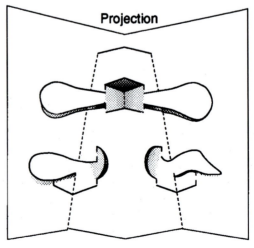

7 CURRICULUM PROJECT

Activity 1 Critical analysis
|
Activity 2
|
engineer form
|
brainstorm themes
|
process three dimensional stages
|
Activity 3
|
personal design stage

Children who have progressed through the horizontal mode of Curriculum Project 5 will find new challenges in Curriculum Project 7 where the skills developed in horizontal engineering are applied to *vertical* pop-up forms. Conceiving pop-ups in the vertical presents a new range of possibilities - anything from cars and monsters to a vase of flowers.

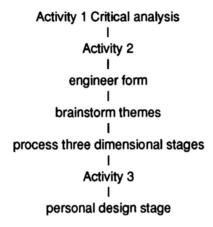
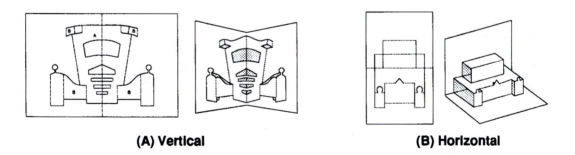

(A) Vertical   **(B) Horizontal**

Activity 1: Critical analysis

Preparation: make a model of a vehicle in the horizontal format (example 'B' above). With the class, compare the horizontal automobile ('B') with the vertical one ('A') you made in the workshop described in chapter 7. In the horizontal model the bodywork is weakened by a flat frontal projection, but this is compensated by the projection of depth. The vertical model has an attractive frontal design but virtually no depth. The reason for this is that variety of formal design is created in the orientation of the folded sections - vertical in the vertical mode, and horizontal in the horizontal mode. Discuss these elements with the class. Lay the vertical model on its side so that the folds are horizontal: now compare these to the horizontal model. Show how the subject matter of the engineering task dictates the design concept.

The Monster
John (aged 10)

*'The primary form in this pop-up represents a head into which secondary form
eyes and moustache have been engineered. The structure is similar to the
Mystical Mountain described in Example 2, but in inversion.'*

Activity 2: Conical Form

Distribute pieces of A4 paper and ask the class to engineer the conical form above. Show how
your Automobile and Mystical Mountain (examples 1 and 2) have 'grown' out of that basic
primary form. Ask the class for ideas and brainstorm possible themes for the two orientations.

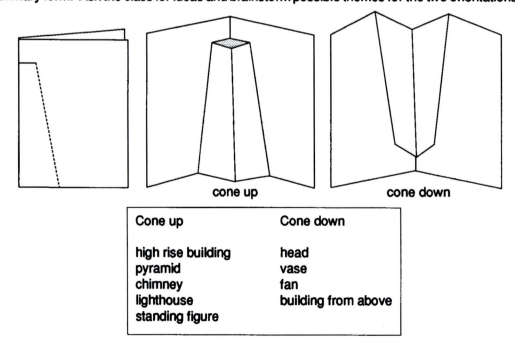

cone up   cone down

Cone up	Cone down
high rise building	head
pyramid	vase
chimney	fan
lighthouse	building from above
standing figure	

Now process three sequential stages with pupils. The cuts required for the pop-up shown in figure 2 can be made with scissors but those in figures 3 and 4 require cutters. This is only a simulation exercise. The secondary forms 'Y' will be spoilt by the conical folds of the primary form passing through them. Developmental work on cartridge paper should attempt to avoid this by designing and cutting on the flat sheet.

2.

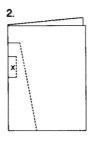
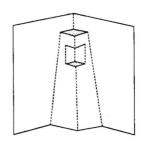

3.

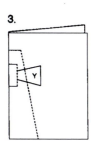
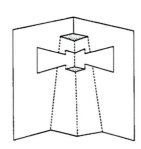

4.

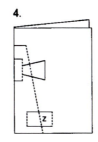
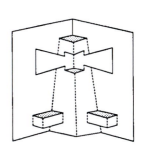

Activity 3: Design

Progress from the test sheets of Activity 1 to a developmental design task. Encourage pupils to sketch pictorial designs and then transfer these to engineering strategies. The style of design should relate logically to the conical form and its secondary possibilities. The diagram opposite shows a basic layout indicating cuts and folds designed to avoid unwanted folds through secondary forms.

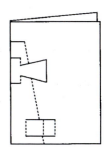

Examples

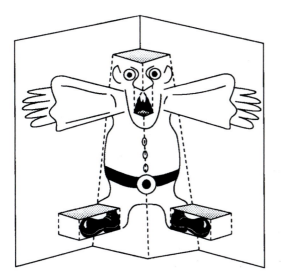

'A giant in boots.'

'A lighthouse.'

The pop-up in the photograph below has been developed from the conical form decribed in activity 2 of Curriculum Project 7. Ellen has followed the "cone down" example. The base of the cone has been conceived as a vase, and the upper portions engineered as flowers.

These flowers are called the: Gondondellia Eating Supper flowers They are a good help sometimes, Because if you've got a piece of cold meat with lots of fat on it and you dont want to eat it the eating Supper Flowers will gobbel it up! (without your Mum knowing) But if you have been

The Gondondellia Eating Supper Flowers
Ellen (aged 10)

'...if you've got a piece of cold meat with lots of fat on it and you don't want to eat it the Eating Supper Fowers will gobble it up!...'

Evaluation

Curriculum Project 7 has taken just one approach to the vertical strategy. There are many others. The main task of evaluation is to assess how successfully pupils have graduated from horizontal to vertical conceptualization and design.

Conceptualization: How well has the vertical strategy been understood? This is inextricably bound up with the pupils' grasp of the appropriate imagery, for one realizes the form through the image and the image through the form. Were the sequential stages of assembly A-B effective using this step by step approach?

Manipulation: Can developing skills in cutting and folding forms be observed? What are the problems for children in both processes and how might they be overcome? Would group activity help those pupils who are struggling with acquiring skills? (For example, 'you hold while I fold'.)

Imaging: How successful were children in creating figurative images to match the conical forms? Could more attention be given to narrative forms to stimulate invention?

Visualizing: The vertical form has a tendency to produce vacant spaces to the left and right rather than top and bottom as in horizontal engineering. Was this characteristic fully exploited in the project's thematic artwork?

8 CONCERTINA FORMS

The Concertina Form is simple, but effective. Like the Run-Away Car and the Mystical Mountain described in Chapter 7, the pop-ups are engineered on the vertical, but out of an extended panel. No sticking and glueing is necessary as the whole design is engineered out of one freestanding concertina form. The concertina can be made as large, or as small as you like - anything from a backdrop for the school play to a colourful birthday card. Children will often be familiar with the concertina from the range of pop-up greeting cards now available in high street shops. There are a number which use the extended panel technique. Bring a few examples to the class, and show the pupils how to make their own.

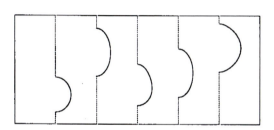 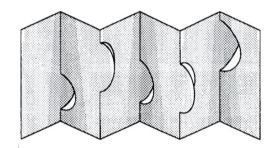

Note that extended sections follow direction of concertina folds.

Experimental forms

A freestanding concertina form on a space theme.

8 CURRICULUM PROJECT

Activity 1: Birthday Card

The concertina curriculum project is suitable for pupils of all ages in groups of any size. One way to approach the project is to distribute several strips of paper to each pupil. Encourage the class to experiment with various pop-up forms before designing the final version. Following blackboard diagrams, pupils mark concertina folds at 6cm intervals and then draw objects which are mainly in the panels but have strategic parts which protrude out of the panels. These extensions are then cut as in the experimental folds illustrated in the workshop. The skill here is to fold the concertina pages *without* the crease passing through the various extended sections.

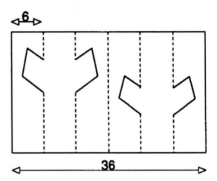

Birthday Card
Chloe (aged 9)

'This project can take as its subject-matter seasonal events, celebrations and special occasions.'

9 TOY THEATRE II

Toy Theatre II is an applied version of Toy Theatre I. The theatre front and stage are made separately and applied to the foundation page. There are two advantages to this method of engineering:

1.   The whole of the theatre interior can be included in the design (no negative spaces);
2.   Using card, a much stronger, durable and larger theatre can be produced.

In addition, Toy Theatre II allows pupils greater scope in their storymaking. Whereas the characters and objects used in Toy Theatre I are engineered out of the back panel, the characters in Toy Theatre II take the form of rod puppets. This opens up a vast range of possible characters and storylines. Characters can be designed in the flat with ease, cut out and stuck onto cardboard rods. They can then be moved in and out of the theatre, allowing pupils to build on the performance skills developed in Curriculum Project 4.

Example: Toy Theatre II

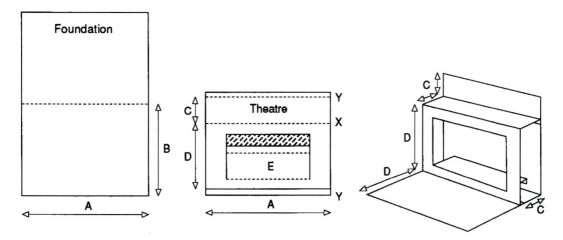

The width of the foundation and theatre 'A' should be the same. Both vertical and horizontal measurements C and D should equate each other. The combined horizontal widths of C and D should equate B. The centre space of the theatre E is engineered back to form the stage and glued to rear foundation panel.

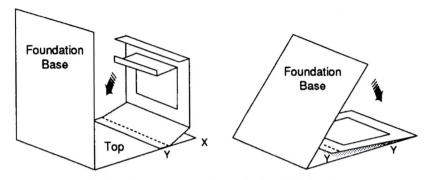

'Glueing the proscenium arch onto the foundation base'

Lay top theatre on top foundation page so that fold X lies flush with the top edge. Glue top flap Y to foundation. Drop theatre down onto foundation and glue bottom flap Y. Drop foundation base down. 'Y' will find its own position on the base. Glue stage into place on the foundation rear panel.

Example 2: Scenery

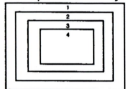

The theatre's scenery should be designed around the story images before it is cut and glued into the theatre. Engineering the three layers of scenery is often one of the hardest concepts in the design stages of Toy theatre II, for it is difficult to conceive on the flat sheet what will be effective in three dimensions. The outer layer, the theatre itself (1) can represent a theatre auditorium, or be the first layer of scenic design. What children have to understand is that each receding layer *must* be visible through the preceding one. Thus, the further back one designs, the less one cuts away (layers 2 and 3). In this way, the theatre gives a tunnelling effect when viewed.

Scenery:

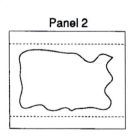 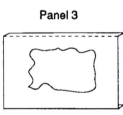 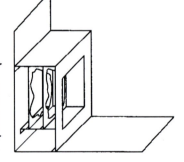

The scenery for the back panel (4) can be drawn straight onto the foundation base. The scenery for panels 2 and 3 is designed and stuck into the theatre on separate sheets. Draw the artwork onto the paper and cut away the negative shapes. Leave a 2cm flap at the top and base of each panel - this will be used to attach the scenery to the theatre.

Lay one scenery panel on top of the other to check the placing of the images. Make sure that the objects drawn on panel 2 do not obscure those on panel 3. Cut away any further areas if necessary. When satisified that you have achieved the desired effect, glue the scenery into the theatre using the 2cm flaps at the top and base of each panel. Toy Theatre II can also be used with moveable scenery. This is engineered in the same way as fixed scenery, but projected from the wings or the flies. In the case of the latter, a slot is cut in the theatre's ceiling before assembly.

9 CURRICULUM PROJECT

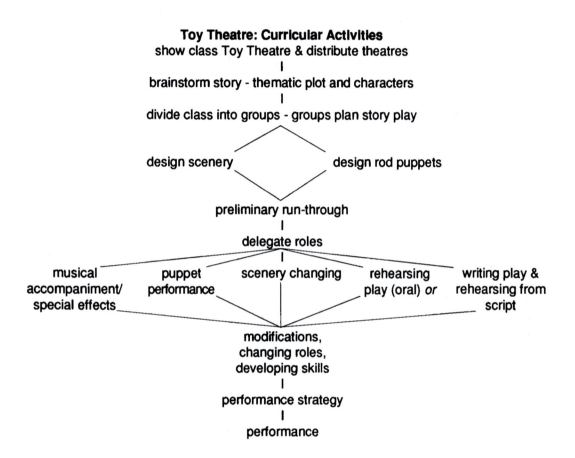

Toy Theatre: Curricular Activities

show class Toy Theatre & distribute theatres
|
brainstorm story - thematic plot and characters
|
divide class into groups - groups plan story play

design scenery   design rod puppets

preliminary run-through
|
delegate roles
|

musical accompaniment/ special effects   puppet performance   scenery changing   rehearsing play (oral) *or*   writing play & rehearsing from script

modifications, changing roles, developing skills
|
performance strategy
|
performance

A whole book could be dedicated to the art and craft of toy theatre rod-puppet production. In the context of this book, coverage is minimal, suggesting possible strategies and starting points for the teacher. Toy Theatre II embraces a whole host of cross-curricular activities. Curriculum Project 9 is a multi-faceted experience, interrelating theatre design, story telling, drama, puppet manipulation and music.

Pre-activity: Making the theatres

Show the class the theatre you have made in the previous workshop. Depending on the age and ability of the pupils, either make yourself, or in collaboration with the children, one toy theatre for each group of about six pupils. Use the multiple making technique described in Curriculum Project 4 in order to save time. Distribute the model theatres to the class.

Activity 1: Thematic exploration

The storyline must be conceived in simple episodic form before the characters and scenery panels can be designed. As a general rule, the story invented should comprise:

1.　one or two main characters who interacts with
2.　one or two secondary characters in
3.　an environment which is in two or three stages.

Brainstorm one or two characters with the class. In order to make the story more interesting, and to avoid cliches, deliberately make these characters seemingly unrelated.

Character 1	Character 2
man	magic umbrella
robot	elephant
denist	ballet dancer
diver	rocket

When a satisfactory pair has been agreed by the groups, they must next establish a situation/ event/confrontation/happening which is the outcome of this unlikely union. This, in itself, should suggest an environment which will form the basis of the first scenery panel.

Activity 2: Group work

Divide the class into groups of about six pupils and ask each group to invent their own version of the story play. It must be sufficiently structured to outline the main characters and their environments. The story may, or may not, be written at this stage.

Activity 3: Delegation of tasks

Delegate the two designing tasks, or allow the delegation to evolve from the groups themselves:

1.　making rod puppets of characters or objects;
2.　making scenery panels.

Pupils make rough designs and then produce card forms from these to make puppets and scenery. Strengthen the rods by applying additional strips of card. Estimate the length of the rod by measuring the distance from centre stage to outside the theatre wings area. Encourage pupils to keep the number of left and right projected puppets equal so that no one side of the theatre is over used.

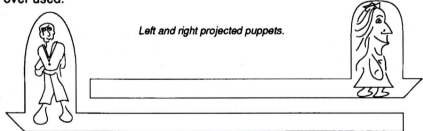

Left and right projected puppets.

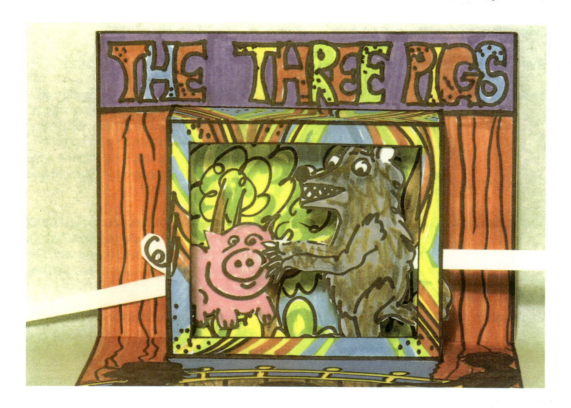

The Three Pigs
Teacher's toy theatre visual aid for a class of 8-year-olds

Activity 4: Developing skills

It is now time for rehearsing the storyplay: refining, changing and restructuring where necessary. Is this to be a memorized oral performance, or one read from a script? The children will need to practice two important moves: first, changing the scenery; and second, moving the puppets (so that pupils do not knock each other's puppets over). The main task at this stage is to decide who-does-what. Will some children have more than one duty, for example, telling the story *and* changing scenery? Is there to be a musical accompaniment (or sound effects) and if so, who is to be responsible for this? Groups can use both tuned and untuned musical instruments to accompany their play.

Activity 5: Performance strategy

The final task before each group performs their play is to decide upon a performance strategy. This will depend upon the audience you have in mind. For example, the class may be producing the play for younger children, and should be encouraged to take that into account in their performance. The curriculum project may be incorporated in a special event for parents. If so, what is the critical response of peer group observers to the dress rehearsal? What changes need to be made, or skills developed further?

Evaluation

There are four main areas to be considered:

Social interaction: How successfully did the group come together? Was the delegation of responsibilities organized effectively? Assess individual's attainments in their specific roles: a) construction, b) performance, and how well they integrated with one another. Was the group dominated by one pupil in particular? If so, was this detrimental to the group and how might it have been avoided? Can you identify pupils whose personal development and self-confidence have been enhanced by the project?

Conceptualization: Did pupils demonstrate suffucient understanding of their specific tasks and how their task fitted into the production as a whole? Did the story have a *shape* and hold together? Were the characters equally well developed? Did the design of the artwork (puppets and scenery) hold the eye, and did they reflect their position in the story play?

Manipulation: How dexterous were puppet performers in manoeuvring the rod puppets in the theatre area? Was there good left and right coordination? Were scenery changes smooth and well organized?

Performance skills: Did the constituent parts of the production fit together? Was the narration/ dramatic dialogue articulated well? What was the reaction of the audiences? How might the production be improved - duration, timing, coordination?

Pupil Evaluation

In my own experience of toy theatre productions there has always been a highly critical awareness during the developing stages - 'No, don't do it like that', 'You're bringing the scenery in too soon', 'We've left out the bit about the Hippo'. As parts of the performance are rehearsed, invite non-participatory members of the team to watch it with a critical eye. Later, groups can compile critiques on one another's performances in the style of a newspaper review.

'I think the first part, up to the house burning down, was good but I got bored in the next part...There were too many puppets on the stage so it got confusing...I liked the chase at the end, but it ended too suddenly.'

(Pupil's newspaper review)

10 ALPHABET BOOK

Alphabeta Concertina
Ron King (Circle Press, 1983)

The Alphabet Book follows directly on from the Toy Theatre II described in Chapter 9. It is, in fact, exactly the same piece of engineering, turned on its side to make a *vertical* form. As with the pop-ups described in earlier workshops, it is largely the thematic imagery that distinguishes horizontal from vertical modes. However, there are some major differences between this vertical structure and its horizontal cousin:

1.   the nature of the design precludes left and right puppet manipulation;
2.   a series of joined vertical theatre forms can be constructed into a standing concertina book. This is not possible with Toy Theatre II.

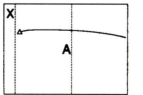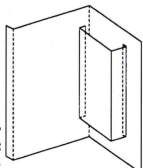

Fold 1cm strip on rectangular sheet A. Fold right side to left folded crease 'X' and fold in half. To prepare pop-up: make height and width 'Y' less than that of base page. Cut, fold, glue fold down and glue again as in Toy Theatre II.

10 CURRICULUM PROJECT

prepare panels and forms
|
pupils process pop-up forms
|
design artwork on the foundation panel
|
design pop-up artwork
|
engineer letter
|
complete artwork
|
glue into foundation
|
assemble alphabet

Alphabet Book

Curriculum Project 10 is a class pop-up book to which everyone can contribute. It is a pop-up alphabet with a letter designated to each child. If the class is larger than twenty-six pupils, some letters can be duplicated or alternatively a separate book made from, say, four letters making a word.

Pre-activity:

The age and ability of the pupils will determine whether you are to prepare the pop-up foundation and rectangles for the class in advance. The alphabet book illustrated overleaf was engineered by a class of eight-year-olds. They followed my blackboard measurements and engineered both sections of the pop-up with little difficulty.

Activity:

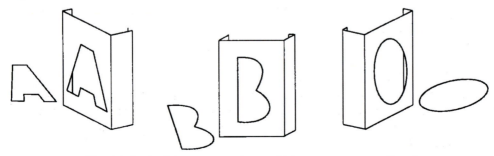

'The alphabet book is a pop-up project to which everyone can contribute.'

A)   When each pupil has a pop-up foundation and rectangle in front of them, allocate the letters of the alphabet in chronological order.

B)   The appropriate letter is then drawn boldly on the theatre panel and carefully cut out. If there are problems with pupils using cutters, make an incision on the letter's form. Pupils can then use scissors at this starting point to cut around the rest of the letter. The central negative spaces of letters like A, B, D, O are not removed. It is important that each pupil keeps the positive cut-away letter for later use.

C)   Now turn your attention to the left-hand panel of the foundation base. This area is to contain an illustration collectively comprising objects starting with the appropriate letter. Brainstorm thematic possibilities with the class: for example, M is for Monkey, climbing a Mountain on Mars. In the project illustrated here, some pupils could only think of one word to make a picture, whilst others integrated six different words. Encourage the class to make their associated objects stand out on the page design, stressing the importance of both colour and shape. Leave blank the area of the foundation page which is covered by the pop-up (see diagram below).

D)   Once the left-hand panel has been designed, colour in the pop-up section and the cut-away letter.

E)   Lift the pop-up form into the right-angle position and place it over the right side of the foundation page. This is the position it will take when it is glued in. Place the cut out letter immediately underneath its negative form and glue onto the foundation panel.

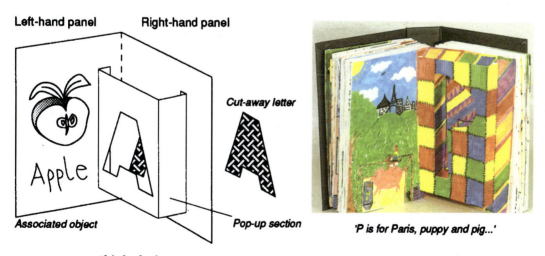

Left-hand panel   Right-hand panel

Cut-away letter

Apple

Associated object   *Pop-up section*

'A is for Apple...'

'P is for Paris, puppy and pig...'

F)   Line up the pop-up section with the right-hand panel of the foundation page, checking the position of the cut-away letter beneath. Glue the strips down side of the pop-up section in place. One is stuck onto the left-hand panel near the central fold, while the other is glued to the right panel of the foundation page.

G)   The final task is to assemble all the letters in concertina fashion. It will now become apparent why the base page has a fold on the left-hand side - this is to glue all the letters together. (The binding method is described in Curriculum Project 5. For an account of more professional book binding methods, see the list of books in the bibliography at the back.)

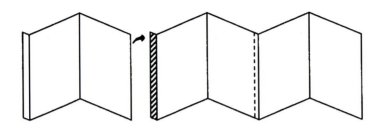

Pop-up Alphabet
Years 10 and 11

Evaluation

Conceptualization and Manipulation:	The skills of cutting, folding and joining introduce a new technique in engineering skills. Drawing letter forms and cutting them out skillfully makes demands on pupils too. Make comparisons between this project and earlier ones involving similar engineering tasks, and record pupils' achievement and progress.
Imaging and Visualizing:	Selecting several objects beginning with the same letter and then designing them into a satisfactory composition is a quite separate task. Compare this with other artwork compositions pupils have produced. Have the drawing and colouring skills developed?

11 THE SPRING

Goofy Dufus
Daniel (aged 9)

*'Goofy Dufus is not the most shy jack-in-the-box you can
find. In fact, last year he won the National Heavyweight
Championships, which is why he is smiling cheerfully.'*

The Spring is the last of the pop-up engineering techniques described in the 90 degree engineering workshop. The concept behind the Spring is similar to that of the Head described in Chapter 2. The innovation is the spring mechanism itself, for it creates an unusual ascending and descending action which children find captivating. Goofy Dufus (illustrated above) is hinged in such a way that his head rises from and descends into his colourful box. Daniel's work forms just one page in an entire book of jack-in-box images assembled by a group of 9-year-olds. Although the jack-in-the-box may be the most obvious choice of character here, experimenting with the shape of the spring can produce a wide variety of images. Alter the angles and you can create Dracula rising from his coffin, or a white rabbit popping out of a magician's hat.

The Spring

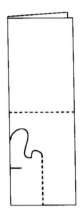

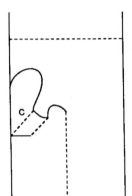

Fold A3 sheet into
four equal sections.

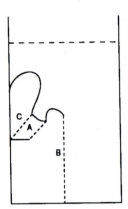

2&3. Cut curve and horizontal line as shown. Crease angle
'A' and fold centre 'B'. (Angles 'A' and 'C' are approx 45°) Fold
down 'A' and fold back again.

4&5. Crease and fold down 'C' and fold back again.

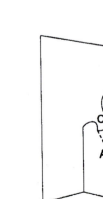

6. Open up page and
drop top flap down
behind engineering.

7. Turn to inside of folded page and project pop-up outwards.
8. Crease 'A' inwards and 'C' outwards and then gently close the page
helping the figure down into the box.

11 CURRICULUM PROJECT

'Although all children progress at varying rates they do tend to follow specific patterns. For example: from simple to more complex and complicated activities and skills; from unplanned and experimental to structural activities; from concrete to abstract ideas and concepts.'

The Lego Education Programme.

The form of the 'spring' is similar to the Head described in Chapter 2, the innovation is the spring mechanism itself. Children may find some preliminary difficulty in engineering this unprecedented technique, but it does create an unusual ascending and descending action which is captivating.

'Experimenting with Spring forms'

Activity:

       The same method as head engineering can be used as an introduction to the technique. If children are following a diagram, keep the basic head and arm shapes simple. Make trials on A4 paper before progressing to A3, or better still, to avoid all project engineering work being the same format, vary the size of the paper used. The illustration in Chapter 11 is just one page in a book of 'Jack in the Box' images assembled by one group of children. The spaces each side of the box provide an ideal area for containing the descriptions of the character portrayed.

Evaluation

The main task to be evaluated is the conceiving and executing of the spring mechanism. How might those pupils who are having difficulties with this be helped? Could small group teaching be useful here? Show how hands, arms, shoulders and head can be made more interesting by drawing the figure first and then analysing the engineered design from that. By engineering on the open, rather than folded page, designs can be assymetrical, thus creating a more inventive design. Which pupils are ready to move on to this more sophisticated approach? Could enthusiasm for this technique be sustained by individuals making a book of spring pop-ups? A story might then relate all the figures in some plot-structured way.

The Mad Monk
Edward (aged 9)

'The Mad Monk walked through the graveyard looking for a fresh grave to rob...'

2 180 DEGREE ENGINEERING WORKSHOP

The completely three-dimensional pop-up

In some respects the experiences gained by the 90 degree workshop will ease the way into 180 degree engineering; but only up to a point. The changes that another 90 degrees make to the constructional science of the genre involve a new mode of thought and design behaviour. In the previous empirical tests it was seen that most 90 degree forms can be assembled from one sheet of paper. This is almost impossible with 180 degree work, and pop-up forms are nearly always applied to the foundation page. Another difference is that the tension between foundation page and pop-up is much greater in the 180 degree mode, because the ascending section has to be hoisted into position through twice the amount of space. The force of gravity is a physical challenge for the engineer, for that which is not constructed on sound paper technology principles will surely collapse!

There must be hundreds of techniques for raising three-dimensional forms off a flat base. In published pop-up books 180 degree models of engineering stimulate the mind and seduce the eye. Yet some of the most visually impressive of them are simply conceived and easily constructed.

Some standard joining techniques are not shown here. For example, a common method of joining a pop-up to its base is to slide it through a slot and glue down to the reverse side of the base. This way, no attachment flaps are seen and, in some cases, the manoeuvrability of the moving parts improved. But whatever the aesthetic and technical advantages, it is a time-consuming method on which to embark. Moreover, if paper rather than card is used, the slots weaken the base and unevenness occurs. It is best, at least at the beginning stages, simply to glue the applied pop-ups down to the page, and that is the technique used here.

There are so many 180 degree forms and combinations of forms that it would be an encyclopaedic task to discuss them all in one book - especially one designed for use with children. I have limited my area of analysis to those basic kinds which are popular in pop-up published books and therefore of immediate appeal to children.

12 THE BACKBONE

The backbone pop-up is probably one the commonest 180 degree forms of them all. As it is primarily a vertical, figure-like shape it can accommodate virtually every image which is essentially upright. A moment's reflection will deduce that this includes almost everything contained on the planet!

The Backbone

From........   to........

'In the form which it is presented first it is seen solely from the front. Later it will be explored in a 360 degree spatial orientation so that one can walk around it like a piece of sculpture.'

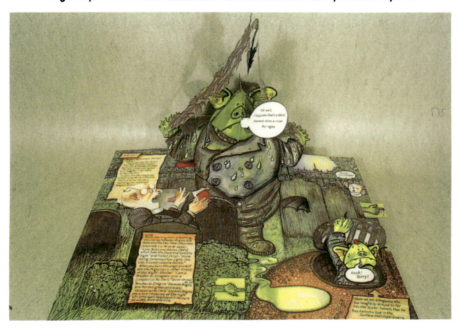

Fungus the Bogeyman
Raymond Briggs (Hamish Hamilton, London 1982)

'The celebrated Fungus is a model of inventive pop-up technology and perhaps the most famous 180 degree pop-up of them all. The page illustrated above combines several different engineering techniques in one figure.'

Stage 1: Basic Primary Form *(not to scale)*

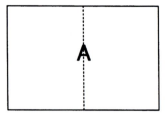

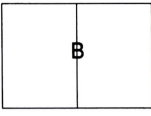

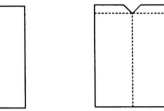

1&2. Take two pices of A4 paper. Fold one in half to be the foundation and cut the other piece in half (A5) to become the pop-ups.

3&4. Fold one A5 piece from 'B' in half. Then cut a diagonal mitre off the corner on the fold and crease mitred flaps.

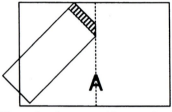

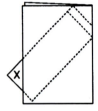

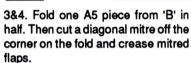

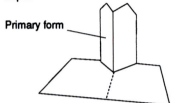

Primary form

5. Align mitred corner with central spine of the foundation and glue down bottom flap.

6. Glue the top flap and drop the right foundation on top. Leave closed and cut off excess area 'X'. Then open page.

The King and the Cat
Rahshid (aged 6)

'The story is written when the pop-up is in place. This in itself is a dynamic stimulation for developing literacy skills.'

Stage 2: Secondary Form

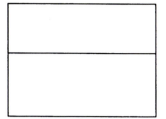

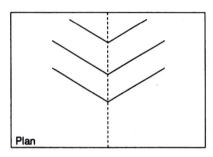

1. Cut the remaining A5 sheet from 'B' into two irregular horizontal strips.

2. Fold the largest piece in half and repeat the mitre process in stage 1.

3. Align the strip with the primary form. *(Approx. 3cm)* and glue down one flap.

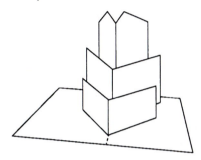

4. After putting glue on the other flap, lift it around the Primary Form before lowering the page. Once the glue has stuck, open page, the process can then be repeated to achieve another secondary form.

5. Any number of secondary forms can be added in this way, providing that none protrudes beyond the edge of the closed page.

Stage 3: Applied Forms

Applied forms can be engineered off primary and secondary forms as shown in the 90 degree workshop in Chapter 6. Ensure that the height of applied form 'X' is no greater than the space from form to edge of base 'Y'.

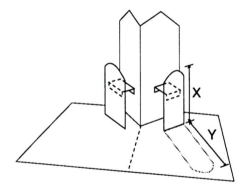

Points to Remember

Avoid angles of 30 degrees or less when joining pop-up to base. Small angles give inadequate 'pull' to the foundation when opening, and the form may flop over.

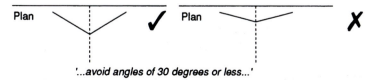

'...avoid angles of 30 degrees or less...'

Experiment with the backbone by cutting away areas in the forms to enhance the shapes and give them specific meanings.

Secondary Forms	Applied Forms
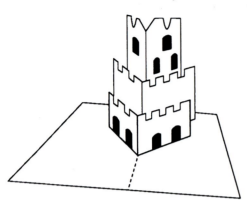	
'...the Castle Keep...'	*'...the Old Lady's House...'*

The Camel
Zafran (aged 5)

'The example above comes from an inner-city infant school. Zafran designed the artwork of the pop-up character and the class teacher glued it onto the page under his direction.'

The 180 degree Arch

Stage 1:

The 180 degree arch is built on the same principle as the backbone, but it introduces two new elements:

1.   the cut away primary form;
2.   the 360 degree spatial design.

Cutting away the centre of the backbone so that two 'legs' straddle the centre spine opens up a whole new range of possible subject-matter. From heads, castles and houses, we progress to tunnels, bridges and the open stage. Prepare the base and primary form as before.

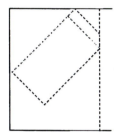  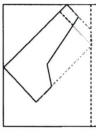 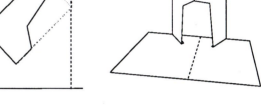

1. Align mitre of primary form with the centre of foundation. Draw lightly around the form.

2. Cut away central area from primary form.

3&4. Lay primary form over pencil outline and glue underneath flap down. Follow stage 1 diagram 6 to complete joining then open page.

Points to Remember

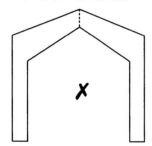 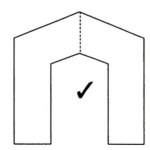 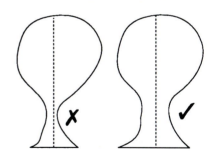

When cutting the central area out of the primary form, do not remove too large an area, as this weakens the structure. In addition, it is important not to allow the base of the primary form to become too narrow, or the pop-up will collapse.

 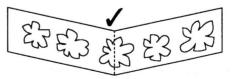

'When designing secondary forms avoid cutting right to the base.'

Example 1: **Outdoor stage and performer**

The outdoor stage and performer combines elements of both the backbone and the cut-away arch with its 360 degree spatial design. Whereas previous examples have been spatial in the sense that the artwork is drawn on the front and back of the forms, here the main form is truly three-dimensional with artwork drawn on the front, back *and* sides.

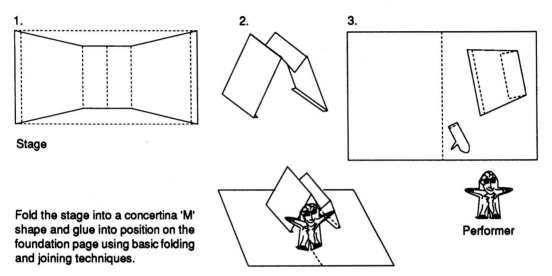

1.

Stage

2.

3.

Fold the stage into a concertina 'M' shape and glue into position on the foundation page using basic folding and joining techniques.

Performer

Pop Festival
Riyaz (aged 10)

'The popstar illustrated above can be seen from both the front and back and stands in an auditorium which has been designed on all sides.'

12 CURRICULUM PROJECT

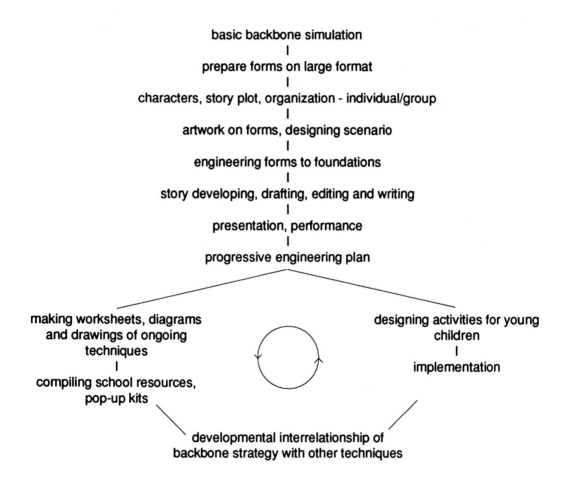

basic backbone simulation
|
prepare forms on large format
|
characters, story plot, organization - individual/group
|
artwork on forms, designing scenario
|
engineering forms to foundations
|
story developing, drafting, editing and writing
|
presentation, performance
|
progressive engineering plan

making worksheets, diagrams
and drawings of ongoing
techniques
|
compiling school resources,
pop-up kits

designing activities for young
children
|
implementation

developmental interrelationship of
backbone strategy with other techniques

Of all the encounters I have had with children in teaching pop-up paper engineering, the backbone structure is the most popular. Perhaps this is because it is so easy to make in its basic form and there are so many things that can be done to change its image.

This curriculum project describes two different activities: the first is intended for use with very young children; the second takes as its model a project carried out with a class of 8- and 9-year-olds. I take as my starting point the work of Daniel (aged 3). His Batman & Robin, Catwoman and the Joker are excellent examples of early 180 degree pop-up engineering. Pictured overleaf, his three-fold concertina book shows how one teacher introduced the Backbone in the nursery.

The Backbone In the Nursery

Daniel's nursery teacher, Margaret, had been on one of my *'Book Art'* courses and when she returned to her class she showed her 3- and 4-year-olds what she had made. Her pop-up models were received with great enthusiasm, and it was not long before pupils wanted to make a pop-up of their own. She showed them how the paper form had been folded and glued on a base and then, hey presto, a pop-up!

Thick paper was distributed and the children were at liberty to draw whatever pop-up image they wanted. They had already experienced concertina books, so Margaret combined the two - a pop-up story sequence in a three-fold concertina book. As figures were completed, Margaret cut around the forms and glued them into the pupil's choice of place. Daniel's Batman (pictured opposite) not only shows how the pop-up form is a stimulus to pre-literate story-sequencing, but also to sequencing on the page. The three characters in the illustration (Batman, Robin and the Batmobile) form a sophisticated juxtaposition of images for a 3-year-old.

Three-fold Concertina Book

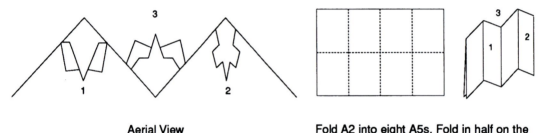

Aerial View

Fold A2 into eight A5s. Fold in half on the horizontal and fold into a concertina.

Activity 1: (for very young children)

Show pupils your own backbone experiments. They will almost certainly want to make one. Prepare suitable foundation pages and provide paper for engineering the primary forms. Discuss themes. Very often images from animated television programmes (like Batman) or stories being read to them will dominate the dialogue. Sometimes, however, memorable events in the child's current experience will be expressed, and all of these form the basis for a pop-up project. Make available art materials and as figures are completed engineer them into the foundation page with the pupils watching and at their direction.

Evaluation

Assess how much of the engineering process children of this age can actually grasp. If several sequences are made, is there any indication that pupils are beginning to approach a stage where they can glue the forms in for themselves? Compare the pop-up work to earlier writing, symbol-making or sequencing. Can any advance be discerned? What do children say about their pop-ups? Can ideas about how you should develop the project be guided by this?

**Batman, Robin
and the Batmobile**
Daniel (aged 3)

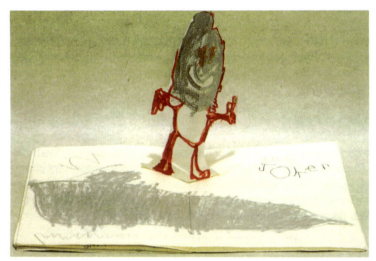

The Joker
Daniel (aged 3)

Catwoman
Daniel (aged 3)

Activity 2:

The organization of Activity 2 bears some comparison with that of Curriculum Project 5, taking as its model a curriculum project which was carried out with a class of 8- and 9-year-olds. Examples of the work they produced are pictured overleaf.

A) Basic backbone simulation

Having been shown a range of published pop-up books as a stimulus, the class was divided into groups of three or four. These became their working groups whenever the project was timetabled. Duplicating paper was distributed, two to a person, and the Basic Backbone Form, (Stage 1) was processed using blackboard diagrams. About half of the class handled this with ease (using scissors rather than cutters) and most of the rest had got to the level of understanding the technique if not quite having the manipulative skills to manifest it by the end of the lesson.

B) Preparation of forms on large format

A3 cartridge was now provided and folded by pupils as their foundation page, and paper was made available for their pop-up forms. Each pupil made the basic backbone primary form using the skills learnt during the previous lesson. All folds and cutting were completed, but none of the forms were glued down at this stage.

C) Formulating characters and story-plot

The groups were now asked to compose a story in three or four parts corresponding to the three or four members in the group. Pupils were told that each part should contain an important image which would become the primary pop-up for each page, but it also had to be linked to the story as a continuous whole. A short improvisory session preceded the group work, in which the whole class took part. This was designed to stimulate the imagination.

For example:

"How can we put a sandcastle, a palm tree and a high-rise building together in a story?"

> "A man is on holiday building a sandcastle, when suddenly the beach exploded. The man swims to a desert island where he climbs a palm tree which grows rare fruit. He eats the fruit which enables him to see into the future. The future is seen as a holocaust with many high-rise buildings on fire."

The paper pop-ups had been prepared prior to the story-making for the following reasons:

1. so that the concrete form of the vertical shape could be present and therefore children could 'see' their image in it;
2. so that once the story had been loosely made, the graphic design process could begin without any delay.

D)   Design artwork

After the story-plot and characters were agreed, the artwork was designed on the primary forms. Pupils were encouraged to cut away parts of the primary form if it enhanced the image. There was, of course, no reason why the whole of the primary form should be used. It would be far more interesting to get away from the stark, rectangular shape. Outlines could be cut by scissors but internal ones demanded cutter work. This particular class were familiar with both scissor and cutter work, but to avoid problems, a cutting table was set aside for pupils who needed to use it and supervised by the class teacher.

E)   Engineering form to foundation

Having designed and cut away their primary forms, pupils were asked to relate them to their chosen environments. Thus, Joleen's sandcastle was positioned on the foundation page and its place marked with a pencil. An area at the front of the page was reserved for writing, but the rest of the base area (allowing for the placing of secondary pop-ups) was left for the artwork. Once final positions had been agreed, the primary form was glued onto the foundation page.

F)   Applying secondary pop-ups

When the primary pop-up had been fixed in place, each pupil sketched a secondary form on rough paper. This had to relate thematically to the primary form. In the examples given here, deckchairs were designed in front of the sandcastle, and tropical plants set out in front of the palm tree. The secondary forms were measured to fit around the primary form, cut and folded. The artwork was drawn on and finally, they were glued into place on the foundation. Some pupils, like Joleen , wanted to add more figures, so the applied 'levered-up' technique was shown to the class and small working groups set up for those who wanted to use it. As you can see from the artwork pictured overleaf, each of the primary and secondary forms has a distinct character of its own.

G)   The Story

The pupils could now stand back from their work and review the imagery and the story which had, at this point, only been discussed in outline. Some new ideas had emerged from the engineering process, so it was time for groups to re-assess the story-plot and re-shape it where necessary. First drafts were exchanged and edited. The main concern at this stage was the continuity between the different episodes. Once each pupil's chosen character and environment had been linked to the next, the final draft was written in the space reserved for it on the foundation foreground.

H)   Presentation, performance and book review

The final stage of the project was a combined 'showing and reading' by each group to the rest of the class. As in Curriculum Project 9 and the Toy Theatres, pupils were invited to watch each presentation with a critical eye. The group work stories were bound into three- or four-sequence pop-up books, complete with cover design and pupils complied critiques of one another's work in the style of a book review.

The Beach
Joleen (aged 9)

'There once was a man on holiday when suddenly the beach exploded...'

The Palm Tree
Catrina (aged 9)

'...he swam to a desert island, climbed a palm tree and ate some rare fruit that enabled him to see into the future...'

The Future
Joe (aged 9)

'...the future is seen as a holocaust with many high-rise buildings on fire.'

Evaluation

Conceptualization: Continuously monitor the progress in acquiring the 180 degree know-how. One common mistake that children make is for the mitred corner to be out of line with the base spine. The page then refuses to lie flat when it is opened. This is a useful mistake for children to make providing they analyse *why* it has happened. Did you make good use of engineering mistakes by asking questions like, "Can anyone tell me why they think Marian's pop-up page does not lie flat when opened?"

Manipulation: The process of attaching forms around existing forms, for example, a beak applied to a primary head, requires considerable skill. Explore progressively, starting with basic primary forms and aiming to arrive at six or more additions. Are pupils working to their level of ability? When should new techniques be introduced? In what ways could pupils working in pairs ease the engineering task? Is adequate provision being made for the less able?

Imaging: There is ample scope for inventing figurative forms to fit the style of basic shapes. Are pupils sufficiently stimulated to investigate suitable images and environments? What kind of visual aids are necessary to show pupils how they might enhance the content of their images?

Visualizing: Marrying the three-dimensional design to the flat base page is an important skill to be monitored. It is so easy for the vertical pop-up to be interestingly designed but the horizontal page to be merely 'coloured in'. How might this be avoided? Can some part of a story be realized on the horizontal area?

'Involvement in the visual and plastic arts should inspire self-confidence and imaginative identification with the culture in which both teachers and children live.'

John Lancaster, *Art, Craft and Design in the Primary School* (NSEAD, 1985)

13 THE CENTRE SPINE

'We want children to consider problems, generate new ideas and develop a wide range of alternative solutions for themselves. Without our deliberately involving them in design and problem-solving processes at school they are less likely to encounter strategies for doing this and less likely to give their creativity vocational relevance.'

Rob Barnes *Teaching Art to Young Children 4-9* (London, Allen & Unwin, 1987)

The Centre Spine is conceptually simpler than the backbone form, but is less versatile.

Stage 1: Basic form

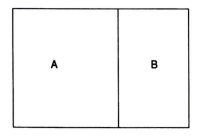

1. Fold an A4 sheet down to A5 as a base. Then divide another A4 sheet into two unequal parts.

2. Fold 'B' in half and crease glueing strips left and right.

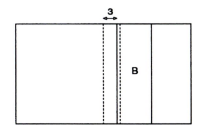

3. Glue folded strip 'B' approx. 3cm from spine on base. Glue top 'B' strip and lower left page to find position.

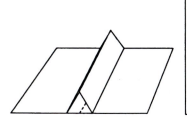

4. Open up page.

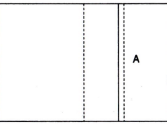

5. Fold 'A' as 'B'. Glue strip to base aligning fold of 'A' flush to right side of page 'X'. Follow step 3. above.

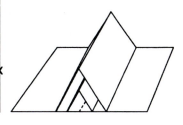

6. Open up page.

Example 1: **Building**

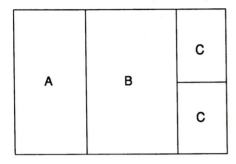

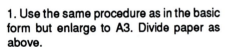

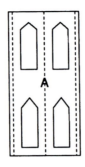

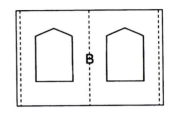

1. Use the same procedure as in the basic form but enlarge to A3. Divide paper as above.

2. On 'A' design and cut out openings.

3. Lay 'B' lengthwise and process as before.

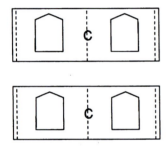

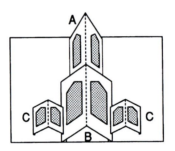

Plan

4. Lay two strips 'C' lengthwise and process as before.

5. Engineer as basic form 3-6 but with 'A' protruding above 'B'. Engineer 'C' each side of 'B'. Use technique described at step 3 to ensure sections do not protrude beyond closed page.

Experiment with alternative forms.

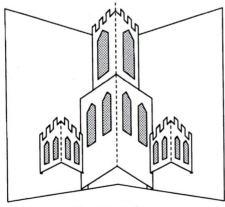

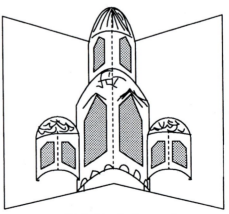

'King Arthur's Court...'

'My holiday in Greece...'

The 'head' centre spine technique is especially suitable for younger children. Why not bind your class' pop-up heads together to make a "Pop-Up Portrait Book"?

The Sad Lady
Mary (aged 7)

'The sad lady is crying becasue someone has taken her sweets away.'

Example 2: **Head**

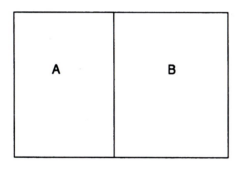

1. Divide A3 into two irregular parts

2. Fold 'A' in half. Cut mouth slit and fold inwards. Crease glueing strips.

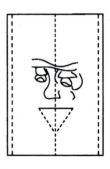

3. Then draw on facial design.

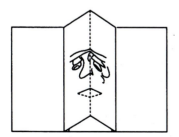

4. Engineer 'A' to base.

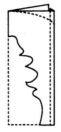

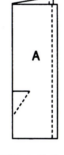

5&6. Cut hair pattern on fold 'B' Then draw on hair, hat, wig, etc.

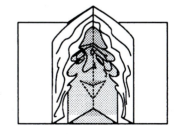

7. Engineer to base, and open page.

Example 3: **Applied beak**

This is another example of a form which could easily be classified under several headings.

Stage 1: Single beak

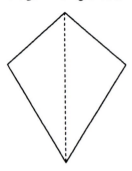

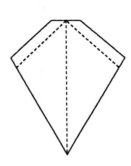

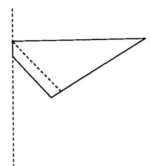

1. Cut kite-shaped form.

2. Remove the top point. Fold strips on top section.

3. Fold in half, glue strips to foundation as in backbone technique.

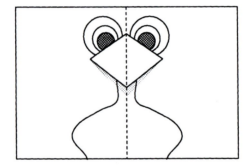

4. Open page...

Stage 2: Double open beak

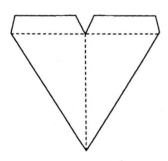

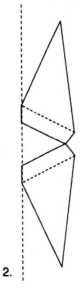

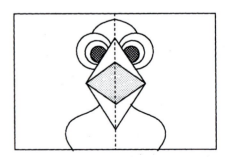

1. Make two triangular shaped forms. Crease, fold and engineer as shown in diagram 2.

2.

3. Open page to project double open beak.

13 CURRICULUM PROJECT

introduce basic technique
|
organize small groups
|
distribute paper sections
|
design artwork
|
check alignment
|
join parts to foundation
|
apply written story

Activity 1:

A)   Use the technique of basic form described in the previous workshop to introduce pupils to the simulation of the centre spine on A4.

B)   This is a project suitable for small group work. Organize into groups of 2 or 3 and distribute A3 either cut into two pieces or uncut, to be prepared by the group. (A3 foundation sheets should be available for collection when required.) The 'cut away' activity must be determined by the nature of the story depicted. Discuss this, for example, if it is a building, what kind of building is it - domestic, castle, factory? Where should the doors and windows be placed? These should be large enough on sections A and B to see through to the far interior on the background. 'A' will probably be the outside of the building, but what is 'B' - an interior wall? If so, how can these inner areas be as interesting in design terms as the facade and far interior? If additional forms are to be used where will these fit - as exterior walls, fences, gates?

C)   Design

Foundation Page   A   B   C

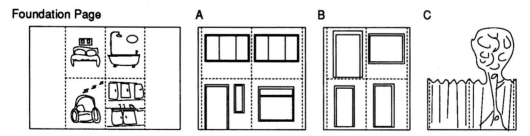

Part B should be aligned on the foundation to define the parameters of the interior area. Doors and windows should match roughly on A and B. As artwork develops A, B and C should be aligned periodically to check superimposed appearance. Can the figures on the inside of the house be clearly seen?

D)   Glue the parts onto the foundation.

E)   The whole group should then invent a story plot to go with the pop-up they have made. In small group work this enables pupils to develop co-operative, leadership and organizational skills. Once a title has been agreed, one member of the group is selected to write the drafted story on the foundation page, or on the back of it.

Evaluation

This is one of the few 180 degree styles in which the whole of the spinal area of the foundation is free of engineering and therefore contains a focal point of the artwork design.

Conceptualization: The design concept is centre-focused. One also looks down on the work rather than seeing it projected vertically into space. Both of these aspects require children to think about the engineering design in a 'tunnelling' way, layers receding one behind the other.

Manipulation: The cutting and glueing process is a relatively simple matter once the positions have been established. Doors and windows which open, rather than completely cut out can make the task more engaging. Assess how successful both the coordinating and cutting of openings have been. Compare this to previous cutting tasks.

Imaging/ Visualizing: Have the groups taken advantage of the house theme and all the colourful things that could go on inside? Are each of the room interiors being designed with the same care and attention? Are the spaces each side of the house an integral part of the design?

The Brown's get a Battering
Meg, Alice, Ben, Harry (aged 10)

'It was pancake day and Adam was making the pancakes but not having a lot of success...'

The story goes on to describe how pancakes eventually went everywhere, even flying out through the window and getting caught up in the trees. Each member of the group had a design role, they were responsible for the story collectively, but only one of them wrote it down on the foundation pages.

Activity 2: The Pop-Up Portrait Book

The 'head' centre spine technique is especially suitable for younger children. Easy to assemble and simple to design, a class of 7-year-olds will enjoy making a head and then inventing a personality to fit it. Show the pupils how to draw the artwork on the two panels - first the hair, or hat, then the face. When the design is complete, glue the panels to the foundation page. The heads can then be bound together in a 'pop-up portrait book'.

Activity 3: Applied Beak

Starlight
Anna (aged 8)
'This is not a normal bird but five metres wide and seven metres tall.
Its beak is as big as a car and eyes as big as a human being...'

The beak design uses the centre spinal area as the focal point of the story. Although I am not generally in favour of children using any kind of templates, this might be an occasion when children drawing round a card shape to produce the beak form would be acceptable. This would particularly be the case with younger children, or those with learning difficulties who, whilst finding the beak concept highly motivating, might not be able to engineer it unaided. Once the beaks have been made, the challenge lies in the artwork itself which has to be designed on both sides of the form. What does the inside of the beak look like? Has the bird got anything in its mouth? Pupils must lay the beak in place to determine its position on the base page so that the mouth interior can be drawn.

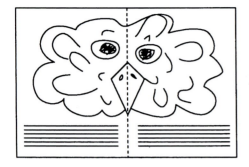

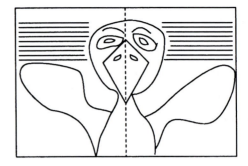

Blackboard Graphics

Blackboard graphics can suggest ways of planning artwork and writing on the flat page. Use the beak position to stimulate imagery, for example, is the bird hungry, and if so, what is its favourite food?

Evaluation

The double open beak requires a certain amount of skill - especially when positioning both beaks so that they fit together. Assess how well this has been done. With younger children (who may have had the whole engineering process done for them) assessment might be concerned with recording the enthusiasm for the artwork and story that the project stimulated. Were pupils keen to make another one? Could this enthusiasm lead to them being responsible for more of the constructing process, even the positioning and glueing?

14 THE TOWER

'Design technology is about designing and communicating, making, testing and evaluating, encouraging children to go beyond their first ideas and seek alternatives so that they may more effectively influence and control the environment in which they live.'

Pat Williams and David Jinks
Design and Technology 5-12
(Falmer Press 1985)

The tower develops out of the centre spine model, but has more scope for invention.

Stage 1: Basic form *(not to scale)*

 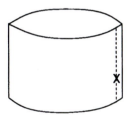 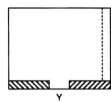

1. Cut a strip from the short side of an A4 sheet and fold a 1cm strip along one edge.

2. Fold left side over to 'X' to form a circle and glue strip to the inside.

3. Fold flat and cut away two 1cm strips leaving section 'Y'.

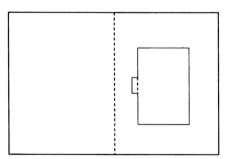 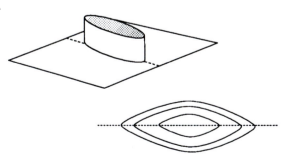

4. Glue underneath 'Y' tab to A4 base approx. 3cm from centre fold. Glue top tab 'Y' down by standard folding technique.

5. Open page... The distance between glued tab and spine determines the shape of the oval tower. (Do not stretch it too far.)

Example 2: **Boat**

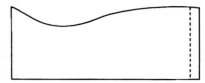

1. Make basic tower form and join together.

2. Modify top contour line to resemble a boat shape.

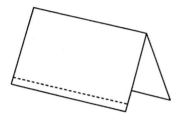

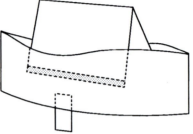

3. Cut out a sheet of paper to make cabin.

4. Fold down in half.

5. Glue cabin down inside hull and add hinges to the hull's sides.

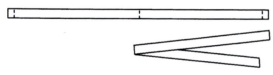

6. Cut two masts and fold in half. It is important that they fit within the page. See diagram 8.

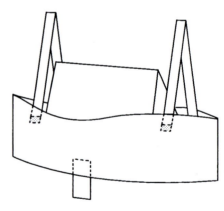

7. Glue the two masts at opposite ends of the hull, on the inside.

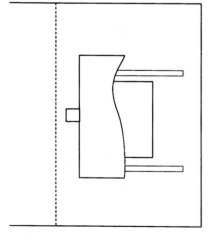

8. Fasten hull hinges to the base as before. Measure available distance between hull and the edge of base page before cutting masts.

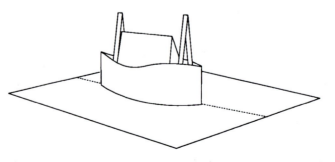

9. Open page.

Example 2: **Bird**

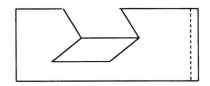

1. Make basic tower shape, join together and cut wing shapes.

2. Fold the wing forms outwards on both sides.

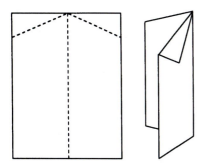

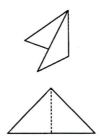

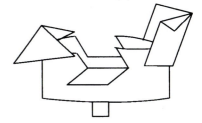

3. Cut a sheet to form head and fold.

4. Cut tail and fold.

5. Attach head, tail and hinges to both sides of the body.

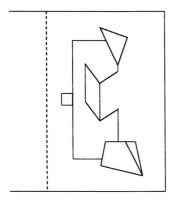

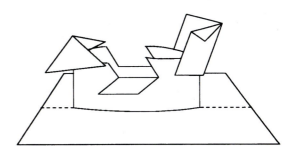

7. Open page to project form.

6. Glue the bird down to the base.

Experiments

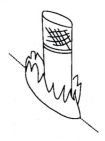

1. A Vase

2. A Kettle or Watering Can

3. A Tree

4. A Lighthouse and Rocks

14 CURRICULUM PROJECT

prepare basic primary form

|

brainstorm imagery

|

design artwork

|

prepare secondary forms

|

design artwork

|

join primary and secondary forms to foundation

|

plan appropriate written work

The basic tower is another form which sits on the foundation spine. Unlike the applied open beak however, one does not 'see' the base inside it for the objects are projected vertically like the backbone form. There are two construction techniques. Secondary forms can be attached to the primary tower before joining into the foundation page (as illustrated in the workshop diagrams), or they can be constructed on the foundation page one at a time. The former method has its advantages for children because they can construct all the sections into one before the final engineering stage.

Activity 1:

A)   Distribute two sheets of duplicating paper to each pupil.

B)   Pupils fold one sheet as the foundation page. From the other sheet they cut a strip and make the tower as described in stage 1 of the workshop. Use blackboard diagrams if necessary to assist pupils during the cutting, folding and glueing process.

C)   The remaining paper is then used to make applied forms. Hold a brainstorming session with the class to suggest the imagery of the tower form they have engineered. Short strips can imply handles, loops, or levers while large ones suggest masts, aerials, or the branches of trees. Very large strips can be made into a ship's cabin, or the contents of a basket.

From these basic experimental introductions pupils should formulate a design for the finished form out of cartridge paper. The trial model will indicate how much paper is needed and what the basic shapes should be. Refinements to the original model should be decided at this stage. Some adventurous pupils may see more complex possibilities in their experiments and want to make a larger construction. Alternatively, pairs or groups can combine their ideas into one collaborative task. Thus, three children all exploring the ship idea might delegate the design tasks as follows:

1. The group discusses the ship theme - haunted ship, fishing boat, cruiser, liner. Is colour to be used, or is the whole form conceived as a piece of super-engineering on white paper?

2. Designer one engineers the hull.
    Designer two prepares the cabin quarters. Are doors, windows or portholes to be cut?
    Designer three engineers the masts, funnel or radar equipment.

3. Periodic 'lining-up' on the foundation page will keep in check the correct size and placing of the forms.

4. After the design tasks have been completed, the whole ship is assembled using one of the two techniques already described.

5. The group examines the form from a 360 degree orientation. Are some viewpoints better than others? Can added accessories like life belts, flags, or people make the design more exciting?

6. After carrying out any necessary refinements to the ship, the group returns to the story. Where is the vessel going, and who is on board?

7. The drafted story is then written in the space around the ship on the foundation page.

| **A Boat on the Water** | **A Party** |
| Katherine (aged 5) | Caroline (aged 5) |

'Two examples of the tower form produced during a curriculum project with a class of infants.'

Evaluation

Conceptualization: The tower is a dominant vertical form. It is seen from every viewpoint. How successfully has its 3D design been achieved? Did the group allow adequate time for discussion about its design and thematic purpose?

Manipulation: How well did the team interact with one another during the assembly stages? Were they able to assist one another? Did they have the dexterity required for glueing forms *inside* the ship's hull?

Imaging and: Ships and boats are exciting things. Do these pop-up vessels attract the
Visualizing eye? Have the groups fully exploited the potential of an ocean liner's regalia, or a fishing boat's paraphernalia?

Pupil Evaluation: To complete the project ask pupils to design a questionnaire to record their achievement, for example, "We worked together extremely well/adequately/ not very well/badly". Once the pupils have completed their questionnaire, assess what their answers tell you about the class.

15 PAPER MECHANICS

The three-dimensional book forms that have been described so far have all been dependent on the hinging faculty of the moving page. Many other kinds of paper engineering are manipulated on the single page itself, and although not pop-ups they belong to the same family. The following chapter shows three developmental uses of the *manually operated lever.* The technique is concerned with lifting a flat form into a spatial orientation.

Stage 1: Levered Theatre

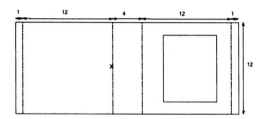

1. Measure in centimetres as above and cut theatre opening.

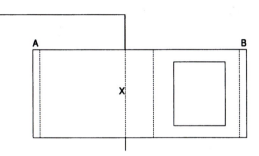

2. Glue strip edge of 'A' to an A4 base, aligning 'X' with the foundation edge.

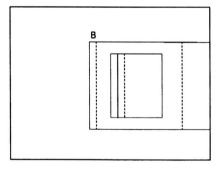

3. Drop theatre panel over and glue 'B' to base.

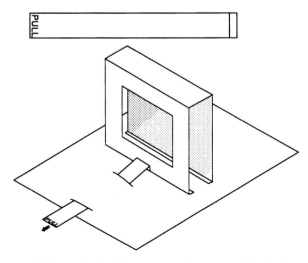

4. Make a 'pull' strip and glue to the base of the theatre front. (N.B. The 'pull' strip is slightly angled.) Slot through two slots in the foundation.

5. The form could be a house, a tent, etc.

Stage 2: **Flapping Wings**

For a successful result use thin card. Keep the foundation page on a flat surface (or presented in book form). If held unsupported the lever tends to buckle outwards when activated.

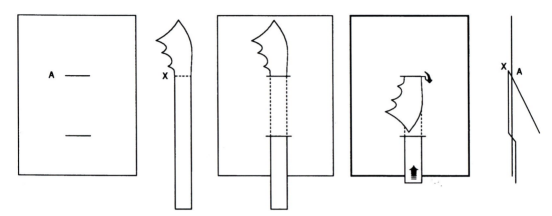

1&2. Make two slots on the foundation page to carry 'pull' strip and make wing form. Crease strip at 'X'.

3. Slot 'pull' strip through foundation page.

4&5. Moving the 'pull' strip activates the wing. For best results the hinge 'X' should be slightly above slot 'A'.

Stage 3: **Door and figure**

At a progressively more intricate level, an opening door and standing figure are lifted from the base simultaneously.

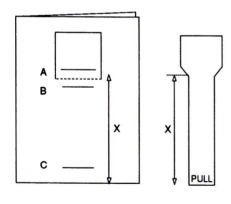
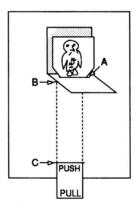
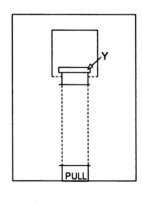

1&2. Fold A3 to A4. Cut door flap in centre of one upper half, hinge at base. Slot 'A' and 'B' lie each side of the hinge. Slot 'C' is situated near the bottom of the page. All these slots are aligned and the same width. Make a 'pull' strip slightly narrower than the three slots. The larger top end should be slightly smaller than the door flap on the base.

3. From above, slot 'pull' strip through slot 'A' on open door, then throgh slot 'B' to the back of page and then out to the front through slot 'C'.

4. Glue small strip of paper 'Y' on the lever under slot 'A'. Up and down movement of the 'pull' strip opens and closes the door revealing and hidding the figure on the inside panel.

The Crystal of Wisdom
Adam and Tom (aged 9)

*'The great explorer went to the Terror Mountain to look for the Crystal of Wisdom.
But the Terror Beast of the lost city found him. There was no hope for him now.
The end.'*

15 CURRICULUM PROJECT

distribute paper
|
demonstrate levered theatre
|
measure theatre opening and cut
|
position theatre strips on foundation page and glue in place
|
attach 'pull' strip to theatre
|
slide 'pull' strip through slots in foundation page
|
design artwork on front and back panels
|
raise theatre to three-dimensional position

Activity 1:

A)   Distribute two sheets of duplicating paper to each pupil.

B)   Demonstrate the Levered Theatre to the class and with the help of blackboard diagrams explain its simple technological principal.

C)   Using your own examples and blackboard diagrams show the class how to measure a theatre opening on one side of their sheet and cut away a panel. By varying the size and shape of the opening pupils will discover that the Levered Theatre can take on a whole variety of possible forms. The cut away panel can leave anything from a proscenium arch to a television set; or a fish tank to a microwave.

D)   Next, pupils glue the strips at the base of the theatre to an A4 foundation page. Show the class how to get the strips in the correct position by aligning one edge of the roof ('X') with the edge of the foundation. It is important that each pupil understands the relation between the positioning of the strips and the final orientation of the theatre.

E)   The 'pull' strip used to lever the theatre into its three-dimensional position should be made of strong paper, or card, and secured (at a slight angle) to the front of the theatre. Younger pupils may require several attempts before successfully glueing the strip in place.

F)   Show the class how to cut slits in the foundation page and slide the 'pull' strip through. If necessary, prepare the foundation page beforehand with the slots already made.

G)   Pupils design the artwork on the front and back panels of the theatre and raise it into place.

The Blurbs
Jonny (aged 10)

'In the deep Amazon forest something stirred. No-one knew what it was, yet... The movement came from a large volcano right in the middle of the forest. Out of it rose two creatures both as horrible as each other. As they rose, tons of bubbling hot lava came cascading down the sides of the volcano. It was the legendary Blurbs.'

The essence of paper mechanics is accuracy of measuring. That alone is not sufficient, of course, because understanding the concepts of the engineering process is essential to success. The Levered Theatre is, by itself, not much of a creative challenge, the inventive element lies in what goes on *inside* the theatre. Its construction, therefore, relies upon the development of technological skills rather than aesthetic ones. Blackboard diagrams can indicate the measuring and folding details to be drawn onto the prepared paper by pupils. The glueing into position is a different matter, for whilst this can be indicated by a diagram, it is more effectively demonstrated by manipulating a model.

This is also the case for the engineering 'push/pull' tab technique which is best learnt by seeing it in operation. The completed theatre can be developed in a number of ways. As paper mechanics are usually engineered on the single page it is one of the few three-dimensional forms which can be worked on with art materials *after* glueing into place. The pulled-up form need not necessarily comprise a theatre story but could be part of a historical project (a famous building, like the Empire State Building in New York); a science investigation (a model of a steam engine); or environmental study (a rainforest). All of these ideas would follow a preliminary simulation exercise so that the finished piece could be designed to match its own particular theme.

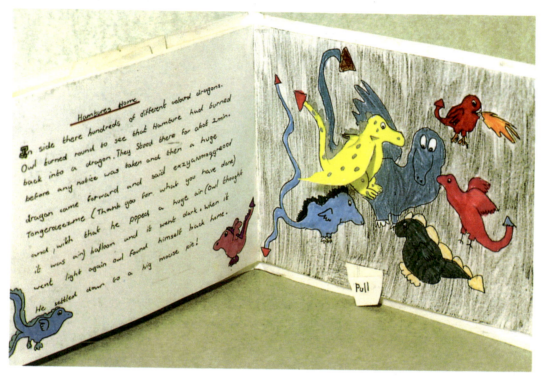

Hamture's Home from Hamture's Adventures
Phillip (aged 9)

Flapping Wings

The Flapping Wings form is really a simple version of the Levered Theatre. To make this activity as creative as possible, simulate the basic task using a rectangular form instead of a flapping wing. This way, pupils will understand that the technique must not be influenced in its design. After all, the top folding down form can be a waving hand, or the oars of a boat. Even conceived as wings, the thematic possibilities are still enormous. They can be the wings of an imaginary flying monster, or the anatomically precise wings of an eagle. Show pupils the basic measurements and shapes on the blackboard, but once this technique has been experienced, however simply, suggest they make a 3D picture book designed to use paper mechanics on every page. The book might be titled "A Book of Wings", or "The Eagle Man". In order to avoid the engineering showing on the reverse side of the wings' page, pupils work on one side only of the folded pages.

16 2D MOVABLES

Numerous mechanical forms are exploited in pop-up books which operate on the flat area of the page. Some of these are swivels which enable objects to rotate or swing from side to side. Characters can be made to disappear and reappear from behind rocks, or climb and descend trees. Levers can operate more than one part of a figure simultaneously, or several different areas of the page. 'Pull' tabs can also operate on front and reverse pages so that two unrelated story sequences can be activated by the same mechanism. There is insufficient space here to even begin to analyse this area of engineering: just two basic techniques are examined.

Basic form

Movable Strip

Foundation

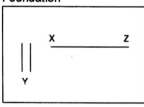

Front

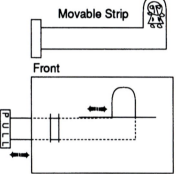

Back

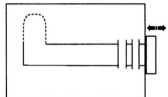

1. The slot 'X' carries the movable strip. Slot the movable strip through 'Y' and glue a 'pull' tab to the end.

2. The length of the movable strip is the same as the distance between 'Z' and the left edge of the foundation.

3. If the strip tends to drop down from 'Y' then add another support slot.

Example 1

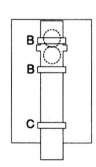
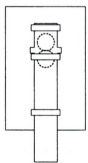

1. Cut a square window in the centre/top of base. Cut a notched movable strip allowing space for two heads corresponding to the window.

2. Lay strip on reverse of base and fasten supporting strips 'B' and 'C'. Align head position.

3. This enables the two positions of the head strip to be opened.

4 &5. Pulling the movable strip down changes the expression on the face from happy to sad.

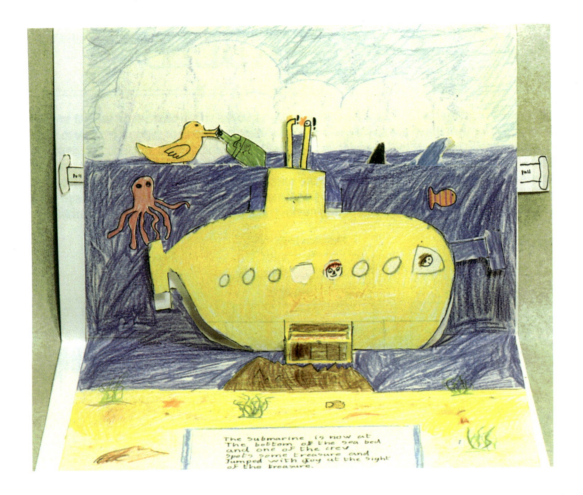

Submarine
David (aged 10)

*'The submarine is now at the bottom of the sea bed
and one of the crew spots some treasure...'*

In this particular piece of work 90 degree pop-up engineering has been combined with two-dimensional moving parts. The submarine pictured above uses three movable strips. Two have been engineered on the back panel and a third has been cut out of the pop-up submarine itself. The seabird with the bottle is pulled from the tab on the left. The shark's fins are moved by the tab on the right.

16 CURRICULUM PROJECT

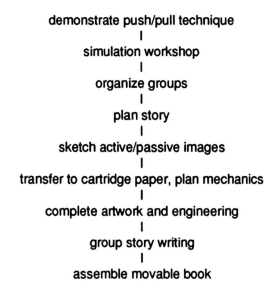

demonstrate push/pull technique
|
simulation workshop
|
organize groups
|
plan story
|
sketch active/passive images
|
transfer to cartridge paper, plan mechanics
|
complete artwork and engineering
|
group story writing
|
assemble movable book

Curriculum Project 16 describes how a two-dimensional movable book was made by a group of 9-year-old children.

Activity 1:

A)   The class were shown a movable book and the push/pull tabs were activated so the story could come alive. There then followed a 'push/pull' simulation workshop in which pupils were given a semi-completed basic form. The slots to the foundation page were already cut, but the children had to cut the movable strip and engineer it in place. The class had worked on a group pop-up project before, so the task of producing a corporate story was not new to them. The room was arranged with children in groups of four. The brief was for them to compose a four-part story as the thematic basis for their movable story book.

B)   From this point onwards, the project will be described through the work of one particular group: Andrew, Ian, Carolyn and Nicola. Ian knew at once he wanted to do a pirate ship, but it took Andrew a while to arrive at his New York skyscraper theme. Of the two girls in the group, Nicola chose a school classroom and Carolyn a graveyard. How these themes would be linked was not discussed at this stage.

C)   A large two-dimensional movable form had been made as a visual aid so that pupils could see, in clear cut forms, how vertical and horizontal strips could be assembled on the same page. The task was to sketch out their page of movable story including at least two movable forms. This necessitated organizing the page into active (movable) and passive (drawn) images and then analysing how these forms would be translated into mechanical operations on the reverse panel. Pupils were also permitted to use other devices like doors, but these will be described later.

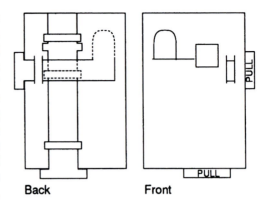

Back   Front

D)   Next came transferring the sketches to A3 cartridge paper and planning the mechanical sections. The movable parts Andrew used were simple. The themes of an aeroplane over New York city and a car on the road were simple horizontal strips. Ian's plot took the aeroplane over the sea where it lands on a ship crewed by pirates. The movable parts in his work are more engaging (see illustration overleaf). At the bottom of the page, cut-out windows reveal the pirates' faces drawn on a movable strip, and at the top of the page, the look-out in the crow's nest is a movable figure. The most ingenious movable part is in the centre where a flag is interchangeable with the 'Jolly Roger'.

Carolyn related her theme of a graveyard full of ghosts to the pirate ship. It had sunk, everyone had drowned and the corpses became the graveyard ghosts. Her movable units were, at the top, an interchangeable sun and moon, and at the bottom, a ghost. There are two hinged covers which reveal other images beneath, tombstones opening to skeletons. (This had been influenced by the hinged doors in Raymond Briggs' *Fungus the Bogeyman*.)

Nicola's story reincarnates one of the corpses, a boy, to act as a link to her classroom theme. But he terrifies the children in the school he visits and they throw their toys in the air. Even the clock on the wall acts strangely. There are three horizontal strips: one of the teddy bear being thrown into the air; another, the teacher writing on the blackboard; and the third, the clock changing time. There are four flaps: three as school desk-tops, and the fourth, the classroom door opening to reveal the born-again boy.

A whole book could be written on the highly creative and scientific activity that characterized the ambience of the room. This was a period of mechanical engineering - cutting openings, making strips, measuring distances, experimenting with manipulating parts (especially where two cross each other), glueing down sections and writing 'Pull' signs. A great deal of shared work went on during this period, as more mechanically-minded pupils helped those who were struggling.

E)   A period of more detailed art work now took place. It was not until some of the engineered parts were in place that the overall surface design of the composition could be completed.

F)   A structured discussion focused attention on the story itself in preparation for its written presentation on the facing page. In all but the first part, this was written on the reverse A4 fold of the engineered page. Using A3 meant that the internal mechanisms of the design were inside the fold, thereby hiding them from view and providing a supporting back page.

A Sunny Day In New York
Andrew (aged 9)

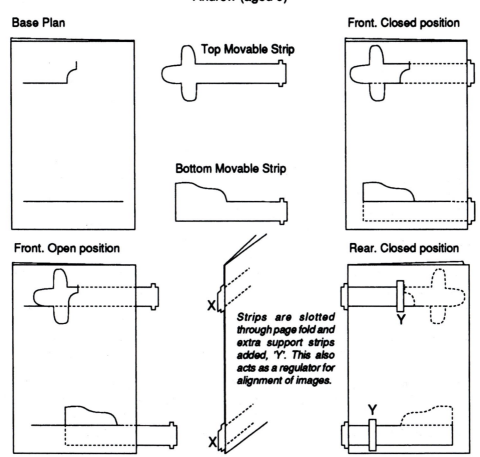

Base Plan

Top Movable Strip

Front. Closed position

Bottom Movable Strip

Front. Open position

Strips are slotted through page fold and extra support strips added, 'Y'. This also acts as a regulator for alignment of images.

Rear. Closed position

The Pirate Ship
Ian (aged 9)

Base Plan

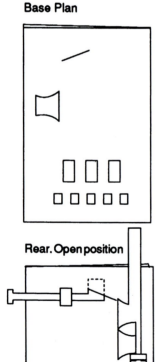

Top Strip

Flag Strip

Bottom Strip

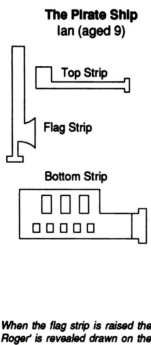

Front. Closed position

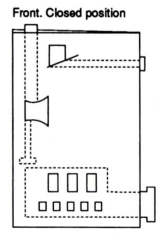

Rear. Open position

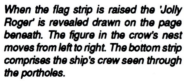

When the flag strip is raised the 'Jolly Roger' is revealed drawn on the page beneath. The figure in the crow's nest moves from left to right. The bottom strip comprises the ship's crew seen through the portholes.

Applied sail on hinge

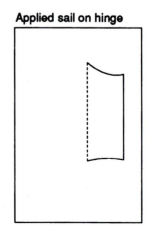

When the Pirate Ship Sank
Carolyn (aged 9)

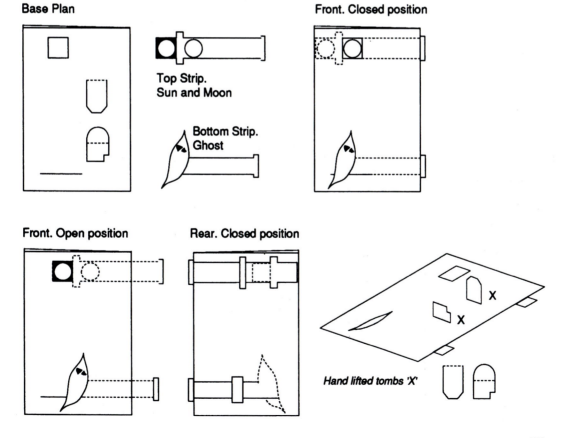

Base Plan

**Top Strip.
Sun and Moon**

**Bottom Strip.
Ghost**

Front. Closed position

Front. Open position

Rear. Closed position

Hand lifted tombs 'X'

School Time
Nicola (aged 9)

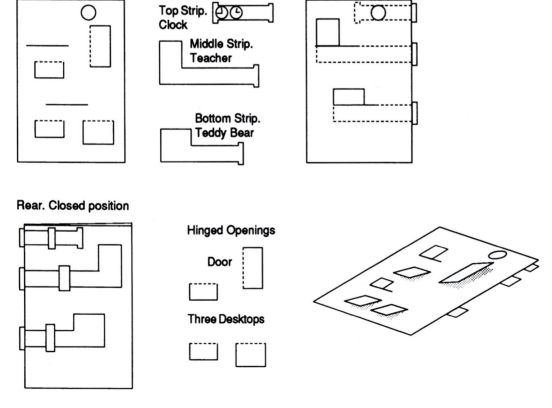

Base Plan

Top Strip.
Clock

Middle Strip.
Teacher

Bottom Strip.
Teddy Bear

Front. Closed position

Rear. Closed position

Hinged Openings

Door

Three Desktops

Curriculum Project 16
Nicola (aged 9)

'Nicola glues one of the three horizontal strips on her classroom scene in place. She has already engineered four flaps: three as school desk-tops, and the fourth as the classroom door.'

Evaluation

Curriculum Project 16 introduces two new engineering skills:

1)   mechanical horizontal and vertical forms;
2)   hand-lifted openings.

Both these techniques are conditioned by the story, and in turn condition the way in which the story develops. Would Nicola's classroom theme have developed in the way it did without the innovation of lifting desktops and a movable teddy bear?

Conceptualization and Manipulation:	Designing strips to coordinate with openings is a new skill to be learnt in this project. For the first time in the curriculum projects most of the work goes on behind the scenes, on the back of the page. Where parts cross over each other at intersecting points, new skills will be needed to prevent them getting tangled. It is astonishing to what lengths pupils will go in overcoming the technical difficulties they set themselves. Look at the engineering on the reverse side of Ian's Pirate Ship page illustrated earlier. Have pupils fully exploited the opportunities for creating moving sections across the page? What were the main problems encountered in the assembly of the units? Was too much expected of the class as a whole, or too little? How might the same project with a different group of children be restructured?
Imaging and Visualizing:	Questioning in this category must concern itself with the relationship between the images and the engineeing strategy. Were pupils familiar enough with the mechanics of the technique to fully realize the story, and *vice versa*? Is there a cohesive linking between the parts of the story? Does the artwork sufficiently exploit the movable medium and how might this be more successfully stimulated in related projects?
Self Evaluation:	This was another project where pupils kept a notebook in which they recorded their ideas and wrote about the engineering possibilities and problems they encountered. The biggest problem seemed to be making the strips move smoothly and to keep their correct positions. What was reassuring was that seventy-five per cent of the pupils said that despite the problems they wanted to make another one!

The success of this movable form is evidenced by the care that has gone into the artwork and writing. The teacher made the foundation page and cut the basic strip but the pupils did the rest. The final stories made an attractive classroom wall display. In fact, the teacher recalls that many examples had to have their movable strips renewed because they wore out from overuse! When the display was removed, the groupwork stories were bound into individual movable books with additional title pages and brightly designed covers.

CONCLUSION

At various stages in the workshops more than one form of paper engineering has co-existed on the page or been suggested in some way. David's Submarine illustrated in Chapter 16 combines 90 degree engineering with two-dimensional moving parts. The ideas expressed in final workshops could be integrated into all of the previous ones. Many of the 180 degree techniques can be assembled on the single hinged page and, as has been seen, vertical structures can have 90 degree forms 'growing' off them.

This has been a book about beginning to discover the language of pop-up engineering, so the interrelation between these forms has not been fully explored in the workshops. The ultimate developmental stage is where both teacher and taught have acquired enough basic skills, and the confidence which comes from that experience, to combine different engineering forms and thereby introduce whole new realms of storytelling and artwork design. Turning the pages of Raymond Briggs' *Fungus the Bogeyman,* one witnesses an almost symphonic design on the two- and three-dimensional surface. It is as if an architectural dimension has been given to storytelling and visual communication. It is at this point, where the poetry of technology harmonizes with the mythological domain of story- and picture-making that the learning lies. The spirit of science and art become one, the desire to make is activated, and children find a unique and indivisible language of their own.

'I used to think that pop-ups were very difficult to make but now that I've made them I think they are not so difficult and that anyone can make them. I think they're the best thing we've done at school this year.'

Rachel (aged 11)

In Chapter 15, the dragon in Phillip's *Hamture's Adventures* was used to illustrate levered mechanical structures. The other pages of the story (pictured overleaf) show just how inspiring paper engineering can be to a child when conceived as a movable book. All the paper mechanisms were processed by Philip and were preceded by trial runs on odd pieces of paper.

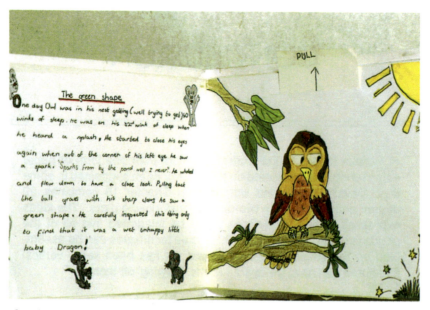

One day Owl was in his nest getting (well trying to get) 40 winks of sleep. He was on his 32nd wink when he heard a splash. He started to close his eyes again when out of the corner of his left eye he saw a spark. "Sparks from by the pond well I never," he hooted and flew down to have a close look. Pulling back the tall grass with his sharp claws, he saw a green shape. He carefully inspected this thing only to find it was a wet unhappy little baby Dragon!

Owl soon found that the dragon's egg had been dropped into the pond. The dragon had hatched and had to swim up to the top without air. "Well we'd better find your mother and father," Owl told him. "Tryie theie pondie," replied the dragon in a high pitched voice. Owl and young dragon (whose name is Hamture) flew high up (well, as high as Hamture could) and dived head first into the pond!

They landed on the bottom of the shallow pond with a thud. A cloud of green and yellow dust covered them. It died away only to see two green frogs (one with a spot on its back). The two green frogs (Owl and Hamture) noticed a strange green door on the pond's bed. It was very stiff but Hamture managed to open it. It was dark inside, but they went through.

Inside there were hundreds of different coloured dragons. Owl turned round to see that Hamture had turned back into a dragon. They stood there for about 2 minutes. Hardly any notice was taken and then a huge dragon came forward and said, "Exzyanmoygreool exzyanmoygerazesezme." (Thank you for what you have done.) And with that he popped a huge air (Owl thought it was air) balloon and it went dark. When it went light again Owl found himself back home. He settled down to a big mouse pie!
The End.

BIBLIOGRAPHY

Design Technology Education

Barnes, R. (1984) *Art, Design and Topic Work 8-13*, London, Unwin Hyman.

Bentley, M. *et al* (1989) *Primary Design and Technology in Practice*, London, Longman.

Design Council, The (1990) *Change in Practice* - Design and Primary Education.

Johnsey, R. (1990) *Design Technology Through Problem Solving*, London, Simon and Schuster.

Lancaster, J. (1991) *Drawing, Designing and Making*, Oxford, Blackwell Educational.

Lever, C. (1990) *National Curriculum Design Technology Key Stae 1-3*, London, Trentham Books.

Tickle, L. (1990) *Design Technology in Primary School Classrooms*, London, Falmer Press.

Williams, P. and Jinks, D. (1985) *Design Technology 5-12*, London, Falmer Press.

Art Education

Morgan, M. (Ed) (1990) *Art 4-11*, Oxford, Blackwell Educational.

Rowswell, G. (1983) *Teaching Art in Primary Schools*, London, Bell and Hyman.

Book Art

Johnson, P. (1990) *A Book of One's Own*, London, Hodder and Stoughton.

Johnson, Pauline (1963, updated 1990) *Creative Bookbinding*, New York, Dover Books.

Pop-Up Book Art

Chatani, M. (1986) *Pop-Up Greeting Cards*, Japan, Ondorisha.

Haining, P. (1979) *Movable Books* , London, New English Library.

Hiner, M. (1985) *Paper Engineering*, London, Tarquin Books.

Children's Writing

Beard, R. (1984) *Children's Writing in the Primary School*, London, Hodder and Stoughton.

Calkins, L. (1986) *The Art of Teaching Writing*, Portsmouth, NH, Heinemann.

Newman, J. (1984) *The Craft of Children's Writing*, London, Scholastic.

Wray, D., Bloom, W. and Hall, N. (1989) *Literacy in Action: The Development of Literacy in the Primary Years*, London, Falmer Press.

Selected Pop-Up Books

Alphabet:

King, R. (1983) *Alphabeta Concertina*, Guilford, Circle Press.

Anthropology:

Hawkey, R. (1986) *Evolution* , London, Michael Joseph.

Architecture:

Smith, D. (1984) *Great Buildings*, London, Purnell Books.

Astronomy:

Couper, H. and Pelham, D. (1985) *The Universe*, London, Random House.

Machines:

Hedgecoe, J. and Meer, R. (1986) *The Working Camera*, London, Angus and Robertson.

Moseley, K. (1989) *Steam Locomotives*, London, Collins.

Reit, S. (1985) *Those Fabulous Flying Machines*, London, Macmillan.

Natural History:

Bantock, N. (1990) *Wings*, Oxford, Bodley Head.

Story Books:

Ahlberg, J. and Ahlberg, A. (1991) *The Jolly Christmas Postman,* London, Heinemann Young Books.

Briggs, R. (1977) *Fungus the Bogeyman*, London, Hamish Hamilton.

Gibbs, B. and Peterkin, M. (1990) *What's in the Bag?*, London, Carnival Books.

Grahame Johnson, A. (illus.) (1983) *Snow White and the Seven Dwarves*, London, Paul Hamlyn.

Griffith, L. *Little Red Riding Hood*, London, Chatto & Windus.

Kubasta, V. (1986) *All at Sea*, Leicester, Brown Watson.

Moerbeek, K. and Dijs, C. (1988) *Six Brave Explorers*, London, Collins.

Moerbeek, K. and Dijs, C. (1989) *When the Wild Pirates Go Sailing*, London, Collins.

Pienkowski, J. (1981) *Robot*, London, Heinemann.

Pienkowski, J. (1981) *Dinner Time*, London, Gallery Five.

Riddell, J. (1980) *Up and Down on the Farm*, London, Atrium Press.

Seymours, P. illustrated by Wallner, J. (1987) *The Three Little Pigs*, London, Viking Penguin.

Strejan, J. and Murphy, C. (1980) *The Incredible Hulk*, Los Angeles, Marvel Comics.

Wells, M. and Kaiser, B. (1986) *Noisy Norman*, London, Blackie & Son.

Welply, M. (1989) *The Magic Toyshop*, London, Collins.

Wyllie, S. and Roffey, M. (1985) *There Was an Old Woman*, London, Methuen.

Wyllie, S. and Axworthy, A. (1986) *The Great Race*, New York, Harper & Row.

Wyllie, S. and Paul, K. (1990) *Dinner with Fox* , London, Orchard Books.

NOTE ON THE AUTHOR

Paul Johnson is senior lecturer in art education at Manchester Polytechnic. He is director of the Gulbenkian Foundation funded *Book Art Project* which has as its main aim the development of children's learning through the book arts. He is a successful paper artist represented widely by galleries in Europe and the United States of America. He has been profiled on BBC television and selected by the Design Council and British Council for exhibitions representing British designer craftsmen abroad. His work is in collections in the United States of America, including the Cooper-Hewitt Museum in New York and the University of California at Berkeley. He is author of *A Book of One's Own* (Hodder & Stoughton, 1990).

CLASSROOM NOTES